BEST OF
BUSINESS
CARD
DESIGN

6

ROCKPORT

ROCKPORT
PUBLISHERS

BEST OF BUSINESS CARD DESIGN

6

works selected by
BLACKCOFFEE

First published in the United States of America by
Rockport Publishers, Inc.
33 Commercial Street
Gloucester, Massachusetts 01930-5089
Telephone: (978) 282-9590
Fax: (978) 283-2742
www.rockpub.com

Library of Congress Cataloging-in-Publication
Data available

ISBN-10: 1-59253-233-0
ISBN-13: 978-1-59253-233-9

10 9 8 7 6 5 4 3 2

Design: Blackcoffee™ • Boston, MA
Cover Image: Scott Goodwin Photography

Printed in Singapore

We'd like to thank all the designers around the world who were willing to share their work. Without such compelling work this book would not have been possible.

We'd like to thank the folks at Rockport Publishers, David Martinell, Kristin Ellison, and Silke Braun for their support throughout this process, as well as photographers Scott Goodwin and Dave Bradley.

Company, Name, Address, Phone, Fax, Email...

In this digital age of laptops, cellular phones, and PDAs, the business card has, ironically, proliferated. More than merely a source of contact information, the business card provides an enticing glimpse into the corporate culture. The more memorable the card, the more memorable the contact.

With the ever increasing competition for eyes, business cards have become more elaborate and sophisticated with each passing hour. Good designers know that limitations exist only in the mind and that some of the most memorable designs are created within some of the tightest budgets.

These unique and innovative cards travel from individual to individual, many times removed from the original recipient. Often these cards make their way into the hands of distant, yet potential, prospects. Such a journey is the product of successful design.

But the greatest of design solutions not only captivate and entice, they clearly communicate with their audience.

The Difficult Task of Choosing

After receiving thousands of submissions from around the globe, the design staff at Blackcoffee chose what they considered to be the best of the best. Contained within the pages of this book are more than four hundred examples of cards that cut through the clutter and successfully communicate information in a legible manner. The judging was based on functionality, communication, and, of course, the wow factor. We hope you'll be wowed as well.

design firm	Blackcoffee
client	Dave Bradley Photography
software/hardware	Adobe Illustrator, Adobe Photoshop, Adobe InDesign
paper/materials	Strobe Gloss
printing	4-color process plus one spot plus satin aqueous

1	
design firm	Blackcoffee
client	Sadie Dayton Photography
software/hardware	Adobe Illustrator
printing	4-color process

2	
design firm	Blackcoffee
client	Neohatch
software/hardware	Adobe Illustrator
printing	1-color PMS plus custom die cut

1

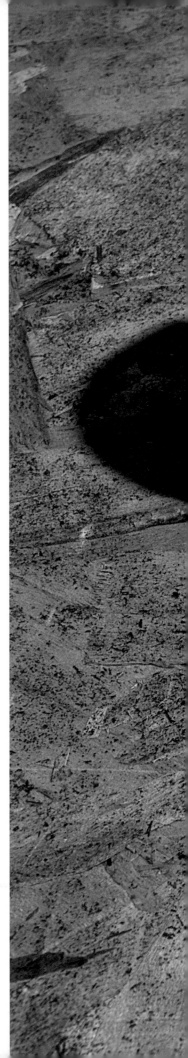

POSITIVE PHOTOGRAPHICS
ACCENTUATE THE NEGATIVE

840 SUMMER ST. BOSTON MA 02127
P [617] 268.6411 F [617] 268.2212
positive.photo@verizon.net

2

design firm	Blackcoffee
client	Nicki Pardo Photography
software/hardware	Adobe Illustrator
printing	4-color process

1

design firm	Blackcoffee
client	Positive Photographics
software/hardware	Adobe Illustrator
printing	2-color PMS

2

clearway

clearway

Vice President of Corporate Communications

Amy Hunt

hunt@clearway.com
Ph: 617.654.6522
Fx: 617.654.6599

31 St. James Avenue Forth Floor Boston MA 02116

3

design firm	Blackcoffee
client	Clearway Technologies
software/hardware	Adobe Illustrator
printing	2-color PMS

3

Erir Read
principal

be.design

eric_read@beplanet.com
1306 Third Street, San Rafael, CA 94901
phone 415.451.3530   fax 415.451.3532

beplanet.com

insight. convergence. presence.

insight. convergence. presence.

insight. convergence. presence.

insight. convergence. presence.

1

1	
design firm	Be.Design
art director	Will Burke
designer	Deborah Smith Read
illustrator	Deborah Smith Read
client	Be.Design
software/hardware	Adobe Illustrator, Adobe Photoshop, Mac G4
paper/materials	Uncoated stock
printing	6 color

2	
design firm	iamalwayshungry
art director	Nessim Higson
designer	Nessim Higson
client	Atomic Pictures
software/hardware	QuarkXPress, Adobe Illustrator
paper/materials	Bonnona paper
printing	Offset

3	
design firm	M3AD.com
art director	Dan McElhattan III
designer	Dan McElhattan III
illustrator	Dan McElhattan III
client	Tamara Foulger
software/hardware	Adobe Illustrator
paper/materials	Protssa Ginger, Superior letterpress—Las Vegas
printing	1 color plus 1 foil

4	
design firm	Hambly & Woolley, Inc.
art director	Barb Woolley
designer	Tony Ponzo
client	Hambly & Woolley, Inc.
printing	2 color plus matte foil deboss

WORTHWATCHING®

a

atomic
PICTURES

BRIAN COLLINS

1314 Cobb Lane, Suite B
Birmingham AL | 35205 | USA
Ⓣ 205.939.1314 Fax 205.939.0585
ATOMICPIX.COM | brian@atomicpix.com

2

m tu w th f sat sun
1 2 3 4 5 6 7 8 9 10 11
12 13 14 15 16 17 18 19
20 21 22 23 24 25 26 27
28 29 30 31

jan feb mar apr may jun
jul aug sep oct nov dec

salon sarjan   2620 regatta dr ste 209b
las vegas, nevada 89128

702 363 1313

TAMARA foulger

702 363 1313

3

130 SPADINA AVENUE, SUITE 807
TORONTO, ONTARIO M5V 2L4
TELEPHONE 416.504.2742 x.24
FACSIMILE 416.504.2745
www.hamblywoolley.com

Hambly & Woolley Inc.

visual communications

BOB HAMBLY partner
bobh@hamblywoolley.com

4

MIASO DESIGN*
KEEP FOR YOUR RECORDS   REF # 30175

MIASO DESIGN*
KEEP FOR YOUR RECORDS   REF # 30175

PRINT WEB
WWW.MIASO.COM
KRISTIN MIASO
DESIGNER
KRISTIN@MIASO.COM   P.O. BOX 31225 • CHICAGO, IL 60631-0225   773.575.3776

1

design firm	Miaso Design
art director	Kristin Miaso
designer	Kristin Miaso
client	Miaso Design
software/hardware	Adobe Illustrator
paper/materials	Init opaque white, French Construction safety orange, factory green, fluse green, 100 lb. cover; glassine envelope
printing	1-color PMS; Award Vision PS, Chicago

The Engine Behind The iT Industry™

Ajunto
Get iT.™
500 n. gulph rd. /ste. 300
king of prussia /pa 19406
610.205.3735 /voice
610.205.3800 /fax
267.254.1698 /mobile
www.ajunto.com

wallace fabian
senior account executive   wfabian@ajunto.com

2

2

design firm	D4 Creative Group
art director	Wicky Lee
illustrator	Michael Hurley
client	Ajunto
software/hardware	Adobe Illustrator, QuarkXPress
printing	3 color

(917) 407 7391
east2thedawn
@earthlink.net

3

rhonda genack

traveling

design firm	Mirko Ilić Corp.
art director	Nicky Lindeman
designer	Nicky Lindeman
client	Rhonda Genack
software/hardware	QuarkXPress, Mac
paper/materials	Cougar
printing	Rob-Win Press

3

4

design firm	plus design, inc.
art director	Anita Meyer
designer	Anita Meyer
client	Rick's Bagel Cafe
paper/materials	French Durotone packaging brown wrap 80 lb. cover
printing	Alpha Press

RICKS BAGEL CAFE
on the street at providence place providence rhode island 02903
phone 401.270.4108 fax 401.270.4884 www.ricksbagelcafe.com

4

David Morton
718.389.0874

BIG TREE

renovation
woodwork
design

source

renovation
woodwork
design

1

design firm	Marty Blake Graphic Design
art director	Marty Blake
designer	Marty Blake
client	Big Tree
software/hardware	Adobe Illustrator, Mac
paper/materials	Mohawk Superfine
printing	Dellas Graphics; Bixler Letterpress; offset, 1 color, letterpress, die cut, blind embossing

2

design firm	Hambly & Woolley, Inc.
art director	Barb Woolley
designer	Dominic Ayre
client	Lucid
software/hardware	QuarkXPress, Mac
printing	2/1 lithography

011010011110100101110

T>240>379>7419
F>240>379>7421
ricekid@ix.netcom.com

Louise Fickel

011LUCID1111010010110

12 South Market Street > Suite 301 > Frederick > MD > 21701

PENTAVARIT

PAUL EVANS

2712 LARMON DR., NASHVILLE, TN 37204 > PHONE: 615.269.6543
FAX: 615.269.6849 > pevans@pentavarit.com > PENTAVARIT.COM

3

3	
design firm	Lewis Communications/Nashville
art director	Robert Froedge
client	Pentavarit
software/hardware	Adobe Illustrator, QuarkXPress
paper/materials	Strathmore laid finish
printing	3 color, 1 side plus die-cut corners

4	
design firm	Roycroft Design
art director	Jennifer Roycroft
designer	Jennifer Roycroft
client	Roycroft Design
software/hardware	QuarkXPress, Mac
paper/materials	Cougar Opaque
printing	Con Kur Printing Co., Inc.

ROYCROFTDESIGN

JENNIFER ROYCROFT

978
475-4504

THREE SHAWNEE CIRCLE, ANDOVER, MA 01810
WWW.ROYCROFTDESIGN.COM
JENNIFER@ROYCROFTDESIGN.COM   FAX 978-475-1455

4

Elisabeth Spitalny Lee
5801 Ostrom Avenue; Encino, California 91316-1451
Telephone: 818.881.3919
Facsimile: 818.881.3913
Email: LeeDesignStudio@mindspring.com

Lee Design Studio

1

1	
design firm	Lee Design Studio
art director	Elizabeth Spitalny Lee
designers	Tesia Rynkiewicz, Elizabeth Spitalny Lee
client	Lee Design Studio
software/hardware	Adobe Illustrator, QuarkXPress
printing	4-color process two sides, satin coating

2	
design firm	Red Communications
designers	Paul Fleming, Curtis Achilles
client	Red Communications
software/hardware	Adobe Illustrator
paper/materials	Classic Crest
printing	2/1

red

CURTIS ACHILLES
curtis@redcommunications.com

155 DALHOUSIE STREET STUDIO 524 TORONTO ONTARIO M5B 2P7
TEL 416.894.2733 « REDCOMMUNICATIONS.COM » FAX 416.214.9569

red

2

Artist

Service

Date & Time

3

B E Y O N D

20 Prospect Avenue
Suite 902
Hackensack, NJ 07601
Tel 201-996-4500

hänan
Middle Eastern Dance | 617.417.0902

3	
design firm	John Kneapler Design
art director	Colleen Shea
designer	Colleen Shea
client	Beyond Spa
software/hardware	Adobe Illustrator, QuarkXPress
paper/materials	Mohawk Tomahawk sage
printing	Infographics; laser die cut at Lasercraft

4	
design firm	Collaborated, Inc.
art director	Tony Leone
designer	Tony Leone
illustrator	Tony Leone
client	Hänan (Amada Berry)
software/hardware	Adobe Illustrator, Adobe Photoshop
paper/materials	Strathmore wove natural white 80 lb. cover
printing	Arlington Lithograph

4

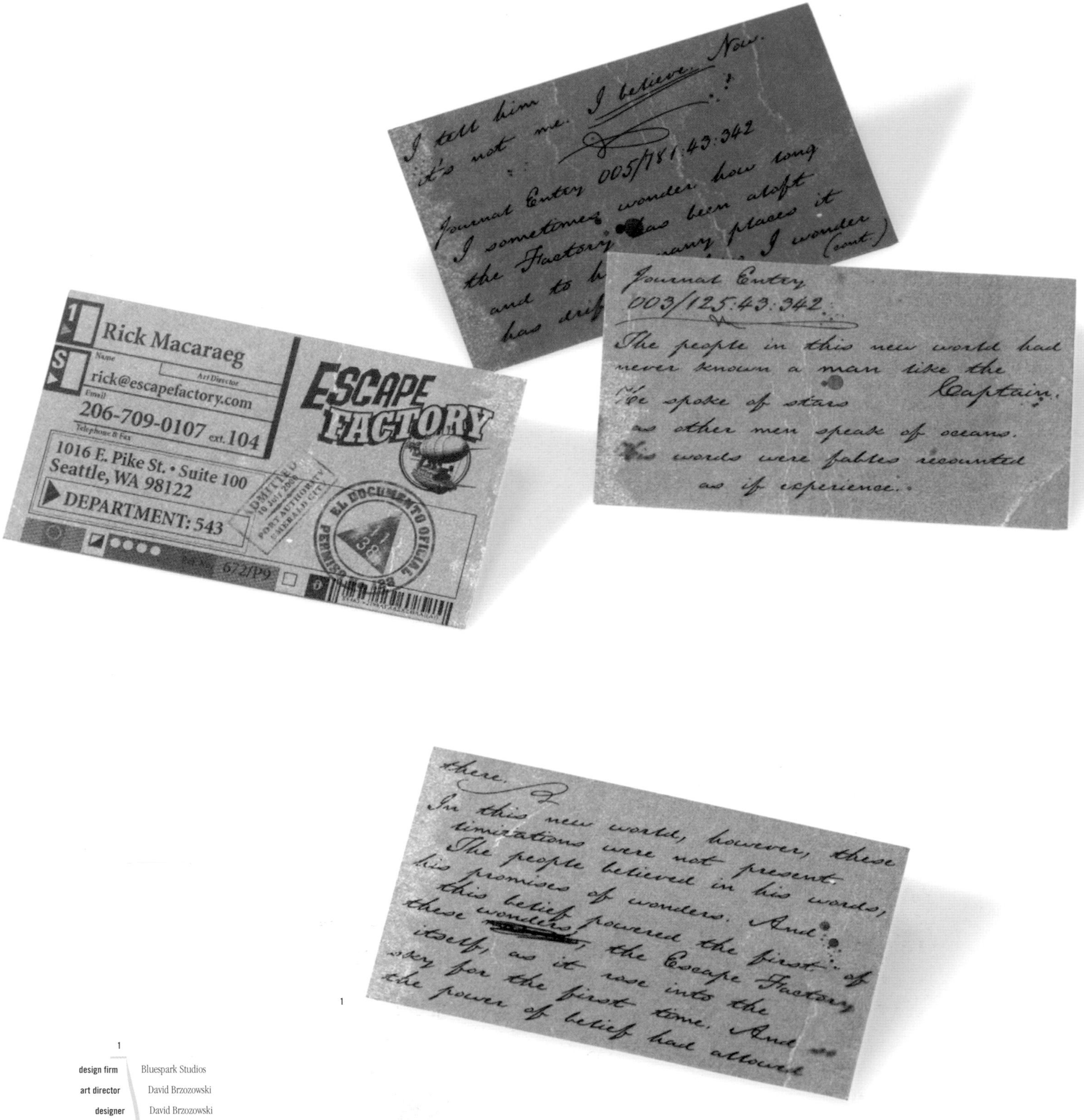

1

1	
design firm	Bluespark Studios
art director	David Brzozowski
designer	David Brzozowski
illustrator	David Brzozowski
client	Escape Factory
software/hardware	Adobe Illustrator, Adobe Photoshop
paper/materials	French Butcher white
printing	3/2

David Titsha
General Manager

Telephone +61 2 9252 0080
Facsimile +61 2 9252 8878
Woolloomooloo Wines
Royal Exchange PO Box R384
Sydney 1225 NSW
Australia
david@woolloomooloowines.com.au
www.woolloomooloowines.com.au

Custodians of fine Australian wine

WOOL
LOO
MOO
LOO
WINES

	2
design firm	Emery Vincent Design
art director	Emery Vincent Design
designer	Emery Vincent Design
client	Woolloomooloo Wines
software/hardware	Adobe Illustrator, Mac
paper/materials	Spicers Star White
printing	Lindsay Yates and Partners

	3
design firm	Wing Chan Design, Inc.
art director	Wing Chan
designers	Wing Chan, Eric Chun
illustrator	Eric Chun
client	Messaging Lab
software/hardware	Adobe Illustrator, QuarkXPress
paper/materials	Classic Crest solar white 110 lb. cover
printing	1 match color

2

messaginglab

3

Karl Schmieder - Principal t 917.913.3396 f 718.499.1713 karl@messaginglab.com

Logo-Entwicklung
Re-Design
Corporate Design
Corporate Identity
Kommunikations-Beratung

THOMAS FABIAN

Wunderburg Design
Innere Laufer Gasse 11
90403 Nürnberg
Fon 09 11-23 55 54 20
Fax 09 11-23 55 54 24
fabian@wunderburg-design.de
www.wunderburg-design.de

design firm	Wunderburg Design
art director	Thomas Fabian
designer	Thomas Fabian
client	Wunderburg Design
software/hardware	Macromedia Freehand
paper/materials	Colorplan, sealing wax, conquerer CX22
printing	Offset

design firm | Brandia Network
art director | Paulo Rocha
client | Brandia Network

1

design firm	Duck Soup Graphics, Inc.
art director	Bill Doucette
designers	Bill Doucette, Sharon Phillips
client	River City Communications
software/hardware	Adobe Illustrator, QuarkXPress
paper/materials	Classic Crest
printing	3 color, embossed logo, die cut

2

design firm	Debenham Design, Inc.
art director	Gareth Debenham
designer	Gareth Debenham
client	Smith & Suita
software/hardware	Adobe Illustrator
paper/materials	Gilbert Esse Smooth

Tailors of Distinction

Tim Horbury
246 Unley Road, Hyde Park
South Australia 5061
Telephone 08 8373 5658
Facsimile 08 8172 2176
Mobile 0418 836 194
tim@tailorsofdistinction.com
www.tailorsofdistinction.com

3

ALLISON KLINE

BUZZBEE

711 NORTH 35TH STREET
SUITE 207
SEATTLE, WA 98103
206 282 4676 T
206 282 4743 F
ALLISON@BUZZBEE.BIZ
BUZZBEE.BIZ

4

3	
design firm	Voice
art director	Anthony De Leo
designer	Anthony De Leo
client	Tailors of Distinction
software/hardware	Adobe Photoshop, Macromedia Freehand
paper/materials	Threads
printing	Queens Court Press

4	
design firm	Ross Hogin Design
art director	Michele Burdon
designer	Ross Hogin
client	Buzzbee Agency
software/hardware	Adobe Illustrator
paper/materials	Fox River Crushed Leaf
printing	The Copy Company

redhat

Michael Johnson
3203 Yorktown Avenue Suite 123 Durham, NC 27713
919.572.6500 x228 FAX 919.572.6726 **www.redhat.com**
johnsonm@redhat.com Red Hat Software, Inc.

1

ON MAIN
7131 EAST MAIN STREET
SCOTTSDALE, ARIZONA 85251
480.947.6042
www.maleesonmain.com

DESERT RIDGE
21001 NORTH TATUM BLVD
STE 44.1380A & B
PHOENIX, ARIZONA 85050
480.342.9220

KRISADA FISHER
CHIEF EXECUTIVE OFFICER

2

1

design firm	Blank, Inc.
art director	Robert Kent Wilson
designer	Robert Kent Wilson
client	Red Hat Software
software/hardware	Adobe Illustrator, Mac G4
printing	G+F Printing

2

design firm	Campbell Fisher Design
art director	Mike Campbell
designer	G. G. LeMere
client	Malee's Thai Bistro
software/hardware	Adobe Illustrator
paper/materials	Environment Duplex cover 120 lb.
printing	1/1, offset

MALEE'S

THAI BISTRO

3

ANDERS MALMSTRÖMER GRAFISK DESIGN
STORA NYGATAN 7 SE-111 27 STOCKHOLM
T08 677 00 84 **F**08 677 00 98 **M**070 772 64 01
A.MALMSTROMER@TELIA.COM
W W W . M A L M S T R O M E R . S E

3	
design firm	Anders Malmströmer Grafisk Design
art director	Anders Malmströmer
designer	Anders Malmströmer
illustrator	Anders Malmströmer
client	Anders Malmströmer
software/hardware	Adobe Illustrator, QuarkXPress, Mac
paper/materials	Uncoated paper 270 gsm
printing	Silkscreen and emboss (hand held)

4	
design firm	Gardner Design
art directors	Bill Gardner, Brian Miller
designer	Brian Miller
client	Bravadas
software/hardware	Macromedia Freehand
paper/materials	Gilbert Essex
printing	Printmaster, 2 color, die cut

4

VaL SiGG

REPRESENTING

d:fi
AMERICAN CREW
alfaPARF
milano
mop
modern organic products

CELL ‹ 316 304 4667
CORP ‹ 888 658 1761

• MODERN SALON SERVICES •
1212 VALLEY RIDGE DR, GRAIN VALLEY, MO 64029

1

design firm	Gardner Design
designer	Brian Miller
client	Val Sigg
software/hardware	Macromedia Freehand
printing	Printmaster, 2 color

2

design firm	Lee Design Studio
art director	Elizabeth Spitalny Lee
designer	Tesia Rynkiewicz
client	Franz Lee Architects
software/hardware	Adobe Photoshop, QuarkXPress
printing	Printed two sides, satin coating, 4-color process

Franz Lee, AIA

5801 Ostrom Avenue
Encino, California 91316

t > 818.881.9906
f > 818.881.9907
c > 310.801.9880

e > FranzLeeArchitect@earthlink.net

Franz Lee Architects
RESIDENTIAL ARCHITECTURE

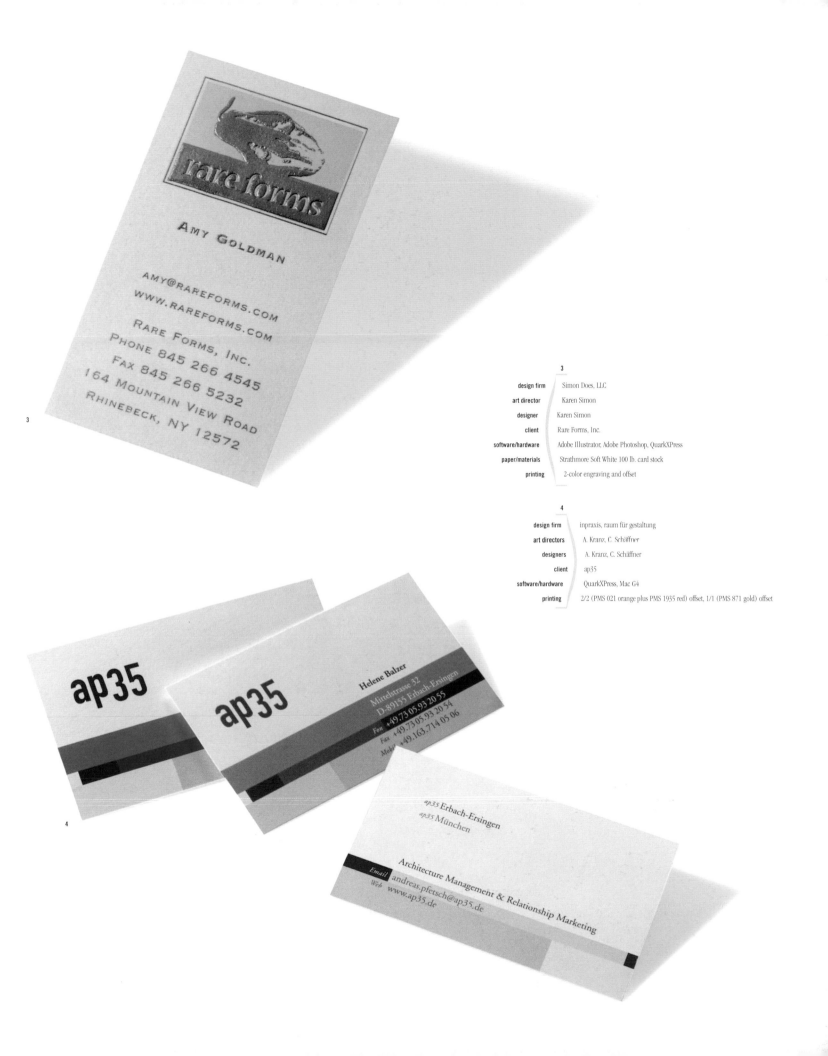

rare forms

AMY GOLDMAN

AMY@RAREFORMS.COM
WWW.RAREFORMS.COM
RARE FORMS, INC.
PHONE 845 266 4545
FAX 845 266 5232
164 MOUNTAIN VIEW ROAD
RHINEBECK, NY 12572

3

design firm	Simon Does, LLC
art director	Karen Simon
designer	Karen Simon
client	Rare Forms, Inc.
software/hardware	Adobe Illustrator, Adobe Photoshop, QuarkXPress
paper/materials	Strathmore Soft White 100 lb. card stock
printing	2-color engraving and offset

4

design firm	inpraxis, raum für gestaltung
art directors	A. Kranz, C. Schäffner
designers	A. Kranz, C. Schäffner
client	ap35
software/hardware	QuarkXPress, Mac G4
printing	2/2 (PMS 021 orange plus PMS 1935 red) offset, 1/1 (PMS 871 gold) offset

ap35

ap35

Helene Balzer
Mittelstrasse 32
D-89155 Erbach-Ersingen
Fon +49.73 05.93 20 55
Fax +49.73 05.93 20 54
Mobil +49.163.714 05 06

ap35 Erbach-Ersingen
ap35 München

Architecture Management & Relationship Marketing

Email andreas.pfetsch@ap35.de
Web www.ap35.de

1

design firm	inpraxis, raum für gestaltung
art directors	A. Kranz, C. Schäffner
designers	A. Kranz, C. Schäffner
client	mbco
software/hardware	QuarkXPress, Mac G4
paper/materials	Clear hard plastic, 0.3 mm
printing	0/2 (silver and green) silkscreen

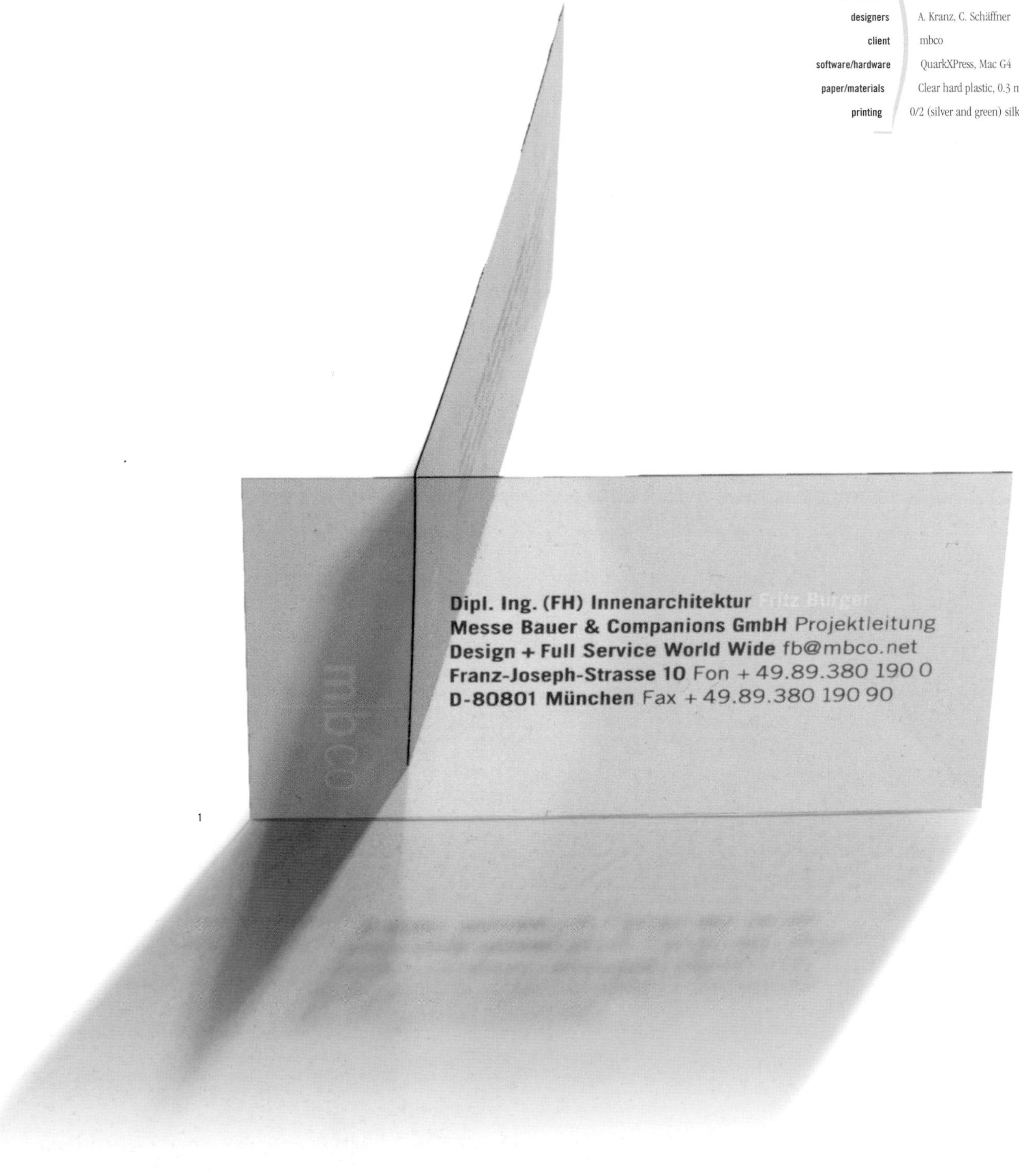

Dipl. Ing. (FH) Innenarchitektur Fritz Bürger
Messe Bauer & Companions GmbH Projektleitung
Design + Full Service World Wide fb@mbco.net
Franz-Joseph-Strasse 10 Fon + 49.89.380 190 0
D-80801 München Fax + 49.89.380 190 90

WWW.SCOTTBAXTERPHOTOGRAPHY.COM

ph: (602) 256-6364
fx: (602) 256-7215

SSBAXTER@MINDSPRING.COM

SB

2

SB

SCOTT BAXTER

PHOTOGRAPHY

1003 EAST SHERIDAN
PHOENIX, ARIZONA 85006

PERFORMANCE GROUP JOE GOODE

MARY JANE EISENBERG
MANAGING DIRECTOR

290A NAPOLEON STREET
SAN FRANCISCO, CA 94124
V 415.648.4848 F 415.648.5401
E JOEGOODE@RCN.COM
WWW.JOEGOODE.ORG

3

2	
design firm	Campbell Fisher Design
art director	Ken Peters
designer	Ken Peters
client	Scott Baxter Photography
software/hardware	Adobe Illustrator, Mac G4
paper/materials	Classic Crest 130 lb. cover
printing	1/1 offset

3	
design firm	Chen Design Associates
art director	Joshua C. Chen
designer	Kathryn Hoffman
client	Joe Goode Performance Group
software/hardware	Adobe Illustrator, QuarkXPress, Mac
paper/materials	Neenah Classic Crest 110 lb. cover
printing	Oscar Printing Co., 1 PMS with blind embossing

1

design firm	Hand Made Group
art director	Alessandro Estera
designer	Alessandro Estera
client	Epica S.R.L.
software/hardware	Adobe Photoshop, QuarkXPress
paper/materials	Business card stock

epica

epica

epica s.r.l.
via venezia,30/32 59013 montemurlo (po) italia
tel + 39 0574 790 931
fax + 39 0574 791 75
info@epicasrl.it
p.i/c.f./impr.po.

epica

epica s.r.l.
via venezia,30/32 59013 montemurlo (po) italia
tel + 39 0574 790 931
fax + 39 0574 791 753
info@epicasrl.it
p.i./c.f./impr.po. n° 01905190979 iscn. rea 481796

i.v.records

CHRIS PARKER President
1701 CHURCH STREET NASHVILLE TN 37203 PHO: 615.320.1444 FAX: 615.320.0750
WEB: WWW.IVRECORDS.COM E-MAIL: CPARKER@IVRECORDS.COM

2

design firm	Lewis Communications/Nashville
art director	Robert Froedge
client	I.V. Records
software/hardware	Adobe Illustrator, QuarkXPress
paper/materials	Strathmore
printing	2 color/1-color blind emboss plus foil

3

design firm	Octavo Design
art director	Gary Domoney
client	Octavo Design
software/hardware	Adobe Illustrator, Mac
paper/materials	White A artboard 360 gsm
printing	2 hits PMS 8422 plus aqueous varnish on both sides

OCTAVO

Gary Domoney
Octavo Design Pty Ltd 42 Eglinton Street Moonee Ponds 3039
Victoria Australia Telephone 613) 8309 8121 Mobile 0425 731 554
Facsimile 613) 9370 2078 Email gary@octavodesign.com.au

3

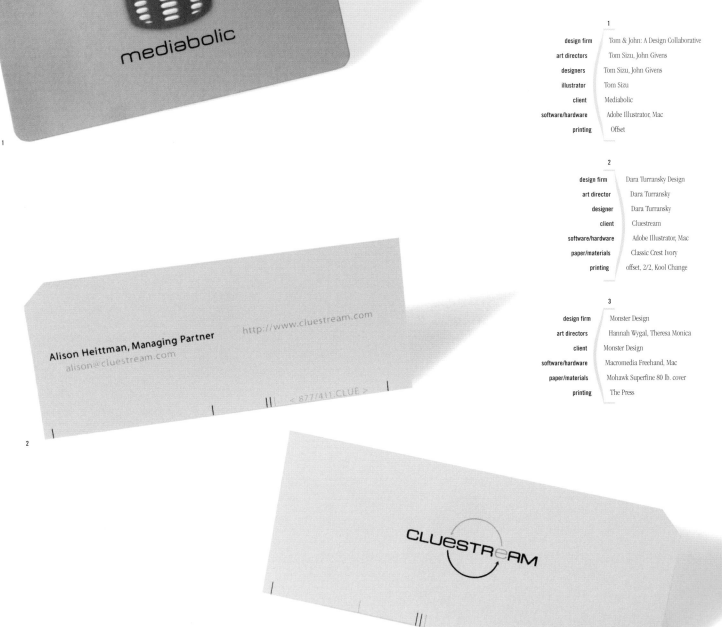

andra indrikis
ART DIRECTOR

1525 UNION STREET. SAN FRANCISCO, CA 94123
TEL 415.346.2270 EXT 111   FAX 415.346.9228
aindrikis@mediabolic.com

mediabolic

1

Alison Heittman, Managing Partner   http://www.cluestream.com
alison@cluestream.com

|| < 877/411.CLUE >

CLUESTREAM

	1
design firm	Tom & John: A Design Collaborative
art directors	Tom Sizu, John Givens
designers	Tom Sizu, John Givens
illustrator	Tom Sizu
client	Mediabolic
software/hardware	Adobe Illustrator, Mac
printing	Offset

	2
design firm	Dara Turransky Design
art director	Dara Turransky
designer	Dara Turransky
client	Cluestream
software/hardware	Adobe Illustrator, Mac
paper/materials	Classic Crest Ivory
printing	offset, 2/2, Kool Change

	3
design firm	Monster Design
art directors	Hannah Wygal, Theresa Monica
client	Monster Design
software/hardware	Macromedia Freehand, Mac
paper/materials	Mohawk Superfine 80 lb. cover
printing	The Press

monsterdesign

hannah wygal

425.828.7853 telephone
425.576.8055 facsimile

hannah@monsterinvasion.com

7826 leary way ne #200
redmond washington 98052

www.monsterinvasion.com

3

4

design firm	Jeff Fisher LogoMotives
art director	Jeff Fisher
designer	Jeff Fisher
client	Slick
software/hardware	Macromedia Freehand, Mac G4
paper/materials	Sundance felt cover
printing	Offset, foil stamping

wendy peck

wendy peck

1346 nw 19th avenue
portland, or 97209
503.224.2556

kristy weyhrich
design director
weyhrich@oh-zone.com

oliver russell
TEL 208 344-2734 EXT 245   FAX 208 344-1211
217 S. 11th street boise id 83702
www.oh-zone.com

1

design firm	Oliver Russell
art director	Kristy Weyhrich
illustrator	Paul Carew, logo
client	Oliver Russell
software/hardware	Adobe Illustrator, Mac G3
paper/materials	Starwhite Tiara 130 lb.
printing	Full Circle Press

1

John Kneapler
President

Tel: 212.463.9774
Fax: 212.463.0478
Email: jkneapler@aol.com

2

design firm	John Kneapler Design
art director	John Kneapler
designer	John Kneapler
client	John Kneapler Design
software/hardware	QuarkXPress
paper/materials	Strathmore white wove
printing	Intographics

2

I'm John Kneapler, the one on the left.
Graphic/Corporate Design, 151 West 19st. #11C
New York, New York 10011 212.463.9774

3	
design firm	IE Design
art director	Marcie Carson
designers	Cya Nelson, Amy Klass
illustrator	Mirjam Selmi
client	IE Design
software/hardware	Adobe Photoshop, Mac G4
paper/materials	Fox River, Select, Warm White
printing	4 color, plus PMS letterpress and die cut

4	
design firm	Entermotion Design Studio
designers	Joe Morrow, Brian Cartwright
client	Entermotion Design Studio
software/hardware	Macromedia Freehand, Mac
printing	2-color screenprinting, enamel ink

3

4

andy martin associates
architects and designers

35-39 old street, london ec1v 9hx
telephone +44 20 7251 1301
facsimile   +44 20 7251 1302
tom@andymartinassociates.com
www.andymartinassociates.com

tom davies
mobile 07775 672239

35-39 old street, london ec1v 9hx
telephone +44 20 7251 1301
facsimile   +44 20 7251 1302
info@andymartinassociates.com
www.andymartinassociates.com

ama

andy martin associates
architects and designers

35-39 old street, london ec1v 9hx
telephone +44 20 7251 1301
facsimile   +44 20 7251 1302
info@andymartinassociates.com
www.andymartinassociates.com

ama
andy martin associates
architects and designers

ama
andy martin associates
architects and designers

35-39 old street, london ec1v 9hx
telephone +44 20 7251 1301
facsimile   +44 20 7251 1302
andy@andymartinassociates.com
www.andymartinassociates.com

andy martin
mobile 07887 506955

design firm   Untitled
art directors   David Hawkins, Glenn Howard
client   Andy Martin Architects
printing   Lithography and foil blocking

MICHAEL LORENZINI

240 Broadway, #301 | Brooklyn, NY 11211 | 718.218.6979 | 347.581.8333 c
www.michaellorenzini.com | ml@michaellorenzini.com

1

STEVE DOMONEY
ARCHITECTURE
42 EGLINTON ST
MOONEE PONDS
VICTORIA 3039
TEL 9372 8207
FAX 9370 3642

2

1

design firm	Nelia Vishnevsky
art director	Nelia Vishnevsky
client	Michael Lorenzini Photography
software/hardware	Adobe Illustrator, Adobe Photoshop
paper/materials	14 pt. glossy card stock 100 lb.
printing	VistaPrint

2

design firm	Octavo Design
art director	Gary Domoney
client	Steve Domoney Architecture
software/hardware	Adobe Illustrator, Mac
paper/materials	White A artboard 360 gsm
printing	2 hits black on both sides, matte film
	lamination, spot UV varnish on both sides

Hey Kookla

Hey Kookla

3

URBAN ANGELIC BOUTIQUE

1025 Montana Avenue   Santa Monica
California   90403
T
inf   F +1 310 899 9477
-kla.com

URBAN ANGELIC BOUTIQUE

Tel +1 310 899 9499

info@heykookla.com

Fax +1 310 899 9477

www.heykookla.com

1025 Montana Avenue Santa Monica California 90403

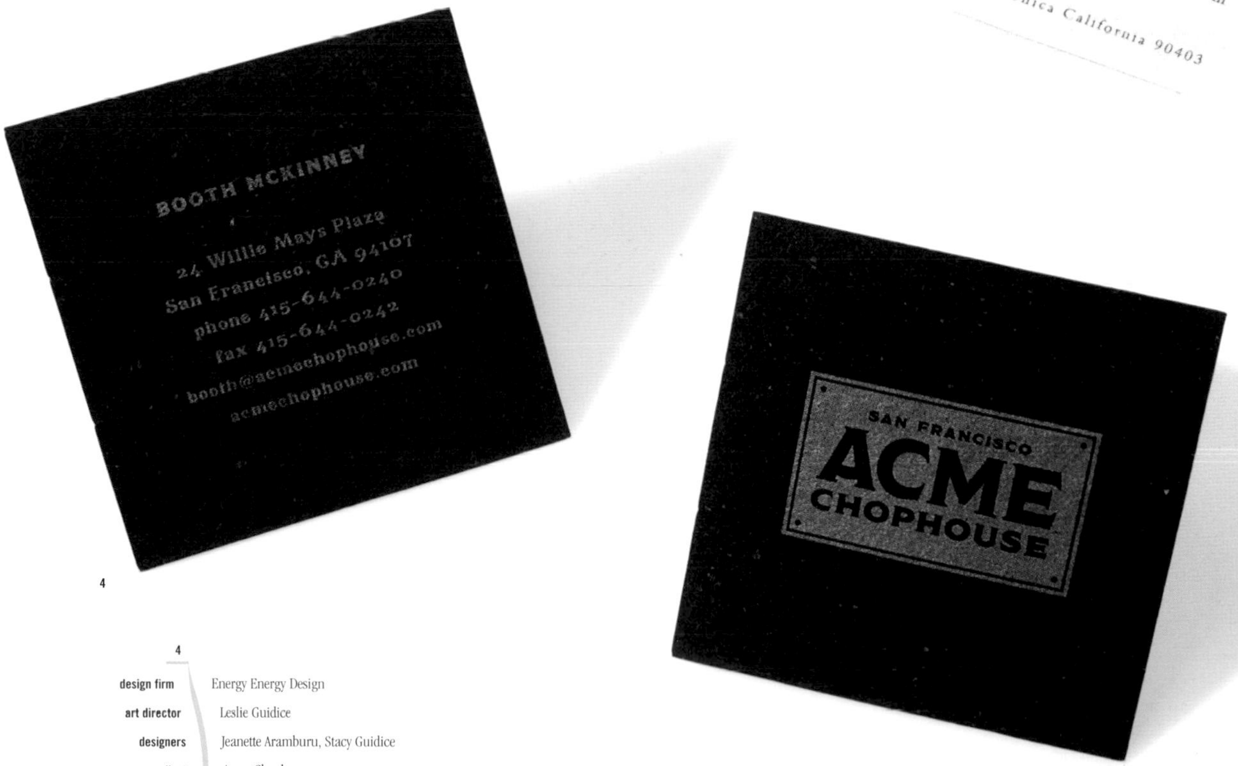

BOOTH MCKINNEY

24 Willie Mays Plaza
San Francisco, CA 94107
phone 415-644-0240
fax 415-644-0242
booth@acmechophouse.com
acmechophouse.com

SAN FRANCISCO
ACME
CHOPHOUSE

4

425 QUEEN ST. W., UNIT 112, TORONTO, ON M5V 2A5, CANADA
Phone.416.977.0088 Fax.416.977.9726 www.change-room.com

David Tam
david@change-room.com

CHANGE  ROOM

" You're switched on! You're smashing! You're shagadelic, baby! "
Austin Powers: International Man of Mystery (1997)

" No price is too high to pay for the privilege of owning yourself. "
Friedrich Wilhelm Nietzsche

425 QUEEN ST. W., UNIT 112, TORONTO, ON M5V 2A5, CANADA
Phone.416.977.0088 Fax.416.977.9726 www.change-room.com

mail@change-room.com

CHANGE ROOM

" To change and to change for the better are two different things. "
German Proverb

425 QUEEN ST. W., UNIT 112, TORONTO, ON M5V 2A5, CANADA
Phone.416.977.0088 Fax.416.977.9726 www.change-room.com

mail@change-room.com

CHANGE ROOM

" Nothing is permanent but change. "
Heraclitus

425 QUEEN ST. W., UNIT 112, TORONTO, ON M5V 2A5, CANADA
Phone.416.977.0088 Fax.416.977.9726 www.change-room.com

mail@change-room.com

CHANGE ROOM

" Sometimes it's the smallest decisions that can change your life forever. "
Felicity (1998)

425 QUEEN ST. W., UNIT 112, TORONTO, ON M5V 2A5, CANADA
Phone.416.977.0088 Fax.416.977.9726 www.change-room.com

Cindy Lam
cindy@change-room.com

CHANGE ROOM

" Of all the things you wear, your expression is the most important. "
Janet Lane

425 QUEEN ST. W., UNIT 112, TORONTO, ON M5V 2A5, CANADA
Phone.416.977.0088 Fax.416.977.9726 www.change-room.com

mail@change-room.com

CHANGE ROOM

design firm	ARTiculation Group
art director	Joseph Chan
designers	Joseph Chan, James Ayotte
illustrator	Joseph Chan
client	Change Room
software/hardware	Adobe Illustrator, Mac G3, G4
paper/materials	McCoy Gloss
printing	Offset

	1
design firm	CHRW Advertising
art director	Dusty Summer
designer	Dusty Summer
client	CHRW Advertising
software/hardware	Adobe Illustrator, Adobe Photoshop, Mac
paper/materials	Neenah Environment natural white 120 lb. cover
printing	Almar Printing

	2
design firm	Campbell Fisher Design
art director	Greg Fisher
designers	GG LeMere, Chris Bohnsack
client	Soma Cafe
software/hardware	Adobe Illustrator
paper/materials	Environment natural white 120 lb. cover
printing	2/2 offset

	3
design firm	Octane
art director	Lee Felch
designer	Lee Felch
client	Octane
software/hardware	Adobe Illustrator
paper/materials	Classic Crest
printing	4/4

	4
design firm	Up Design Bureau
art director	Chris Parks
designer	Chris Parks
client	Penalosa Jerky Company
software/hardware	Macromedia Freehand, Mac G4
paper/materials	House coated cover 100 lb.
printing	Towanda Press

3

4

1		
design firm	Sciortino Advertising	
art director	Jacquelyn Rinaldi	
designer	Jacquelyn Rinaldi	
illustrator	Jacquelyn Rinaldi	
client	Butterfly Group	
software/hardware	Adobe Illustrator	
paper/materials	C2S	
printing	Colour Concepts	

2		
design firm	plus design, inc.	
art director	Anita Meyer	
designer	Anita Meyer	
client	Fifteen Beacon	
paper/materials	Crane's Crest florescent white 110 lb. cover	
printing	Artcraft	

BUTTERFLY

GROUP

GEORGE KING
MANAGING PARTNER

1

LAS VEGAS OFFICE
4955 South Durango Blvd.
Suite 218
Las Vegas, Nevada 89113
T 702.933.3332
F 702.933.3335

NASHVILLE OFFICE
1008 South Clubhouse Court
Franklin, Tennessee 37067
T 615.308.2133
F 615.595.7865

E-MAIL

dwallace@butterflygroup.net

XV
BEACON

2

PAUL ROIFF
president

FIFTEEN BEACON
15 beacon street
boston massachusetts 02108-2902
direct 617.697.6945
telephone 617.670.1500
fax 617.670.2525

3

design firm	Tracy Design
art director	Jan Tracy
designer	Anthony Magliano
client	David Morris Photography
software/hardware	QuarkXPress
paper/materials	Color coated gloss 80 lb.
printing	4-color offset

4

design firm	Inovat Design
art director	Doug Logan
designer	Doug Logan
illustrator	Doug Logan
client	Doug Logan
software/hardware	Adobe Illustrator
paper/materials	Card stock

design firm	Northbank
art director	Simon Cryer
client	Nick Smith Photography
paper/materials	Chromalux 700
printing	4-color process

Nick Smith
Photography
nick.smith13@virgin.net
M 0973 392001

Nick Smith
Photography
nick.smith13@virgin.net
M 0973 392001

Nick Smith
Photography

nick.smith13@virgin.net
M 0973 392001

Nick Smith
Photography

50 Bradford Road
Combe Down
Bath BA2 5BY

T 01225 835125
nick.smith13@virgin.net
M 0973 392001

Images overleaf:
Childs + Sulzmann, architects
Childs + Sulzmann, architects
Childs + Sulzmann, architects
Mann Williams, structural engineers
Childs + Sulzmann, architects

Corporate Clients:
NatWest Life
Prudential
Greig Middleton
GE Capital
Lloyds TSB
Liberfabrica/CPI Group annual report
Granada annual report
HTV West annual report
BSkyB
Crest Homes PLC
SGI (Daily Mail Group)

Hotels and Restaurants:
The Bath Spa Hotel
Caterer and Hotelkeeper magazine
Forte UK
The Halcyon Hotel, London
The Royal Crescent Hotel, Bath
Hotel du Vin, Bristol
City Inn, Glasgow/Birmingham/Bristol

Architectural:
Future Heritage, property developers
Childs + Sulzmann, architects
Mann Williams, structural engineers
Stanhope PLC, property developers

General:
The Countryside Agency
Explore @ Bristol
National Osteoporosis Society
The Bath Spa Project
The Arnolfini, Bristol
The Earth Centre, Yorkshire

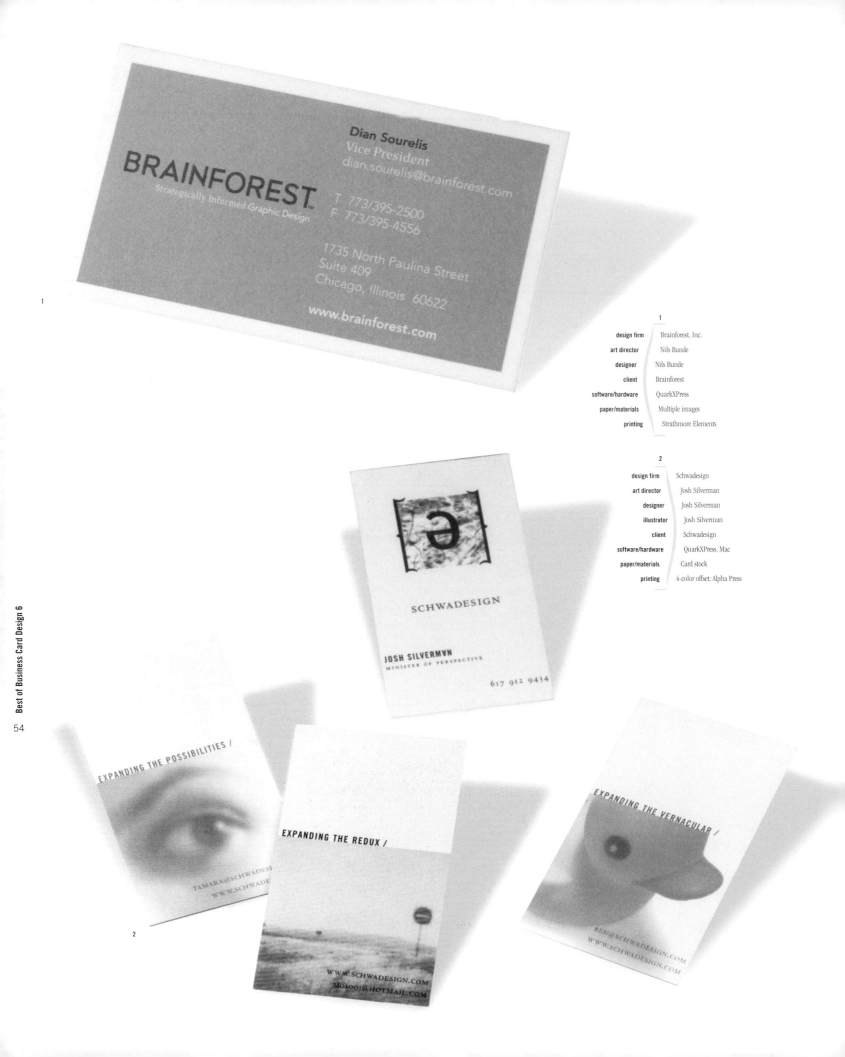

Dian Sourelis
Vice President
dian.sourelis@brainforest.com

BRAINFOREST™
Strategically Informed Graphic Design

T 773/395-2500
F 773/395-4556

1735 North Paulina Street
Suite 409
Chicago, Illinois 60622

www.brainforest.com

1

design firm	Brainforest, Inc.
art director	Nils Bunde
designer	Nils Bunde
client	Brainforest
software/hardware	QuarkXPress
paper/materials	Multiple images
printing	Strathmore Elements

2

design firm	Schwadesign
art director	Josh Silverman
designer	Josh Silverman
illustrator	Josh Silverman
client	Schwadesign
software/hardware	QuarkXPress, Mac
paper/materials	Card stock
printing	4-color offset; Alpha Press

SCHWADESIGN

JOSH SILVERMΛN
MINISTER OF PERSPECTIVE

617 912 9434

EXPANDING THE POSSIBILITIES /

TAMARA@SCHWADESI...
WWW.SCHWADE...

EXPANDING THE REDUX /

WWW.SCHWADESIGN.COM
MO1001@HOTMAIL.COM

EXPANDING THE VERNACULAR /

BEN@SCHWADESIGN.COM
WWW.SCHWADESIGN.COM

TEL/FAX 602-331-1419 CELL 602-738-2239 EDSWEET@PIPELINE.COM

3

A B C D Edward F G H I J K L M N O P Q R Sweet T U V W X Y Z

design firm	Campbell Fisher Design
art director	Ken Peters
designer	Ken Peters
client	Edward Sweet and Associates
software/hardware	Adobe Illustrator, Mac G4
paper/materials	Classic Crest cover 130 lb.
printing	2/2 offset

4

design firm	Energy Energy Design
art director	Stacy Guidice
designer	Stacy Guidice
client	SG Jewelry
software/hardware	Adobe Illustrator
paper/materials	Utopia blue white silk 150 lb.
printing	Next Press

5Gjewelry est.2002 CRAIG G
333 Santana Row Suite 230
San Jose California 95128
P415.309.9127 www.5gjewelry.com

4

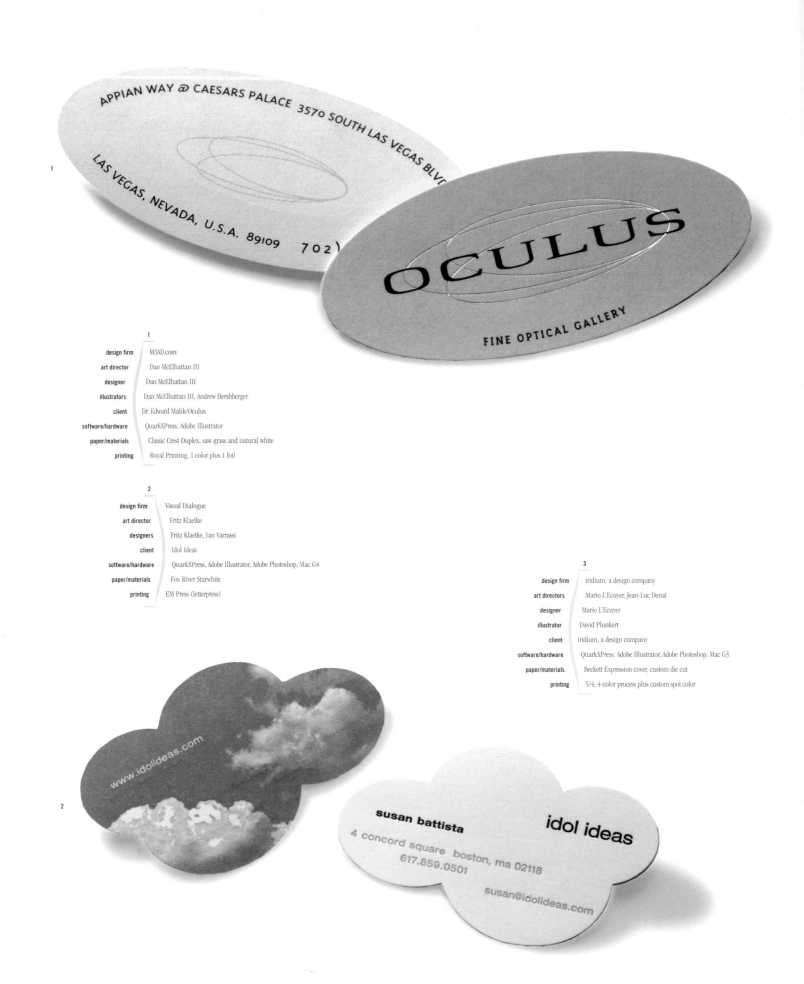

1

design firm	M3AD.com
art director	Dan McElhattan III
designer	Dan McElhattan III
illustrators	Dan McElhattan III, Andrew Hershberger
client	Dr. Edward Malik/Oculus
software/hardware	QuarkXPress, Adobe Illustrator
paper/materials	Classic Crest Duplex, saw grass and natural white
printing	Royal Printing, 1 color plus 1 foil

2

design firm	Visual Dialogue
art director	Fritz Klaetke
designers	Fritz Klaetke, Ian Varrassi
client	Idol Ideas
software/hardware	QuarkXPress, Adobe Illustrator, Adobe Photoshop, Mac G4
paper/materials	Fox River Starwhite
printing	EM Press (letterpress)

3

design firm	iridium, a design company
art directors	Mario L'Ecuyer, Jean-Luc Denat
designer	Mario L'Ecuyer
illustrator	David Plunkert
client	iridium, a design company
software/hardware	QuarkXPress, Adobe Illustrator, Adobe Photoshop, Mac G3
paper/materials	Beckett Expression cover, custom die cut
printing	5/4, 4-color process plus custom spot color

IOP

i on
ink PAPER

William W. Hadley
bhadley@ink-on-paper.com

TOLL FREE OFFICE
866·883·4390
866·883·4389 FACSIMILE
307·690·3035 CELL DIRECT
247 ASPEN LANE
ALPINE / WY / 83128
www.ink-on-paper.com

{DAVID MORRIS PHOTO}

ROSAN CAUBLE

913+ T 432-8860
F 432-2958
3105 MERRIAM LANE
KANSAS CITY, KANSAS 66106
DDMPHOTOGRAPHY.COM

1

design firm	Matter
art directors	Rick Griffith, Jason C. Otero
client	Ink on Paper
software/hardware	Adobe Illustrator, Adobe Photoshop, QuarkXPress
printing	4-color offset (opaque white under color)

2

design firm	Tracy Design
art director	Jan Tracy
designer	Anthony Magliano
client	David Morris Photography
software/hardware	Adobe Illustrator
paper/materials	Classic Crest Columns Duplex
printing	2-color offset

MATT HERRON Chief Technology Officer
matt@outbursttech.com

Outburst Technologies
3170 Cowper St. Palo Alto, CA 94306
t 650.464.3100 f 650.843.1602
www.outbursttech.com

OUTBURST

smart RADIO

3

Evidence™

Evidence™

Evidence™

TELEPHONE 303 477 2820

Daniel R Perales dan@studioevidence.com
2820 NORTH SPEER BOULEVARD DENVER, COLORADO. 80211

FACSIMILE 303 477 8687

4

www.studioevidence.com

	3
design firm	Anvil Graphic Design, Inc.
art directors	Laura Bauer, Roy Tazuma
designer	Cathy Chin
client	Outburst
software/hardware	Adobe Illustrator, Power Mac G4
paper/materials	Strathmore Writing pasted cover ultimate white 110 lb.
printing	Full Circle Press
	4
design firm	Matter
art directors	Rick Griffith, Jason C. Otero
client	Evidence
software/hardware	Adobe Illustrator, Adobe Photoshop, QuarkXPress
printing	3-color offset, blind emboss

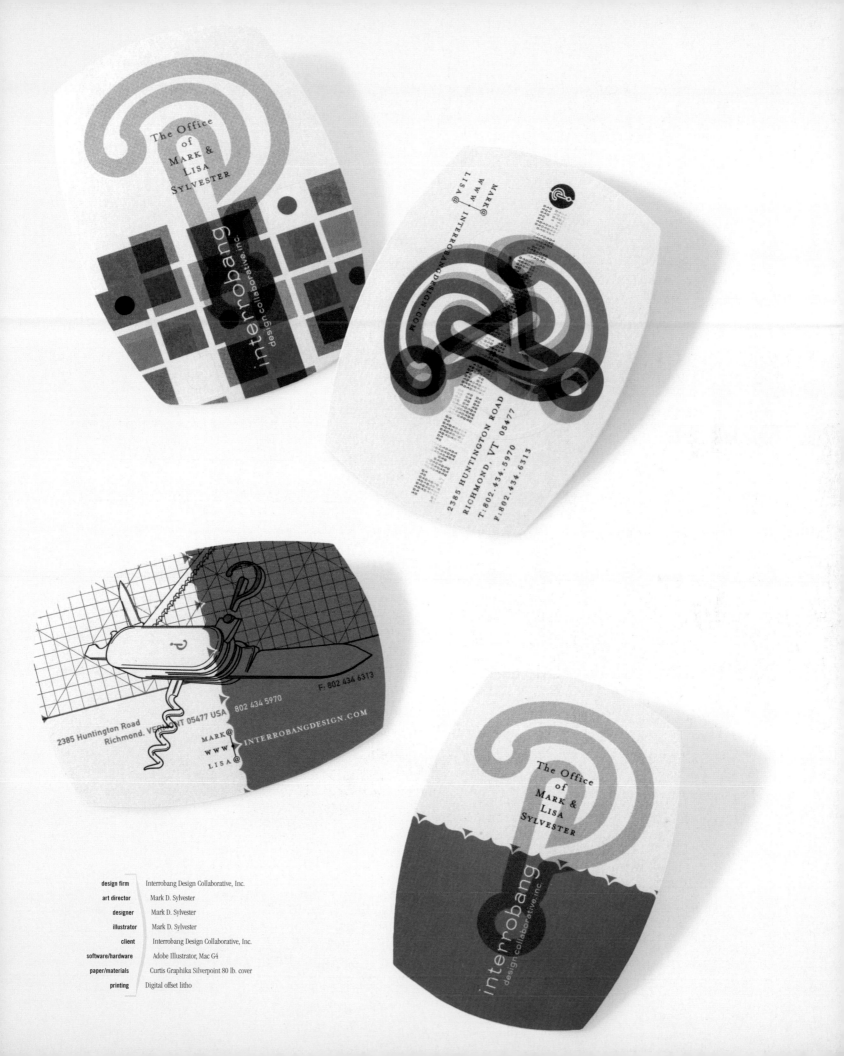

design firm	Interrobang Design Collaborative, Inc.
art director	Mark D. Sylvester
designer	Mark D. Sylvester
illustrator	Mark D. Sylvester
client	Interrobang Design Collaborative, Inc.
software/hardware	Adobe Illustrator, Mac G4
paper/materials	Curtis Graphika Silverpoint 80 lb. cover
printing	Digital offset litho

design firm	Mirage Design
art director	Mark DaPonte
designer	Lynette Allaire
client	Mirage Design
software/hardware	Macromedia Freehand

1

design firm	plus design, inc.
art director	Anita Meyer
designers	Anita Meyer, Karin Fickett, Dina Zazcagnini, Matthew Monk, Nicole Juen, Carolina Senior, Veronica Majlona
client	plus design, inc.
paper/materials	Chipboard
printing	Sun Hill Press

2

design firm	Marius Fahrner Design
art director	Marius Fahrner
designer	Marius Fahrner
illustrator	Marius Fahrner
client	HL Engineering Motors
software/hardware	Macromedia Freehand
paper/materials	IGEPA Extra 250 gsm
printing	2-color offset

MY

FIVE STAR

CHEF

Gourmet cooking
at your place

3

LARRY MICHAELS
Chef/Owner

★ ★ ★ ★ ★

No. 619 890.1159
Hm. 858 456.2772

larry@myfivestarchef.com
WWW.MYFIVESTARCHEF.COM

3

design firm	Miriello Grafico, Inc.
art director	Ron Miriello
designer	Dennis Garcia
illustrator	Dennis Garcia
client	My Five Star Chef
software/hardware	Adobe Illustrator
paper/materials	Neenah Classic Crest solar white
printing	Streeter Printing

4

design firm	Gardner Design
art directors	Bill Gardner, Brian Miller
designer	Brian Miller
client	Tallgrass Beef
software/hardware	Macromedia Freehand
printing	Printmaster, 3 color

TALLGRASS
BEEF®

Pasture-raised on the
family ranches of

TALLGRASS PRAIRIE PRODUCERS CO-OP

telephone/facsimile: 316-273-8301

R.R. 1 Box 53
Elmdale, Kan.
zip code 66850

1-800-992-5967

4

e-mail: tallgrss@valu-line.net

KITCHEN K

A DESIGN GALLERY

1436 U STREET NW, SUITE 100 WASHINGTON, DC 20009
WWW.KITCHENK.ORG PH 202.232.2675 FX 202.387.6596
ALI KOOISTRA GALLERY MANAGER ALI@KITCHENK.ORG

design firm	Kinetik
art directors	Beth Clawson, Jeff Fabian, Beverley Hunter
designers	Mike Joosse, Natalie Politts, Katie Ratsch, Scott Rier,
	Katie Roland, Sam Shelton, Jenny Skillman
client	Kitchen K: A Design Gallery
software/hardware	QuarkXPress, Mac
paper/materials	Mohawk Superfine
printing	Offset

	1
design firm	Zucchini Design Pte. Ltd.
art director	Tew Sun Ne
designer	Tew Sun Ne
client	Ann Chong
software/hardware	Macromedia Freehand
paper/materials	Cromatico, -Ca shocking pink 200 gsm
printing	Octogram Pte. Ltd.

	2
design firm	Sayles Graphic Design
art director	John Sayles
designer	John Sayles, Som Inthalangsy
illustrator	John Sayles
client	Strategic National Retail Group (SNRG)
software/hardware	Adobe Illustrator
paper/materials	aluminum
printing	Screen printing, offset printing

timespin

Gunther Schöbinger

visual design

tel. +49-(0)3641-35 97 26
fax. +49-(0)3641-35 97 11
mobil. +49-(0)172-35 58 501
g.schoebinger@timespin.de
www.timespin.de

timespin
digital communication gmbh

sophienstrasse 1
07743 jena
germany

3

3

design firm	timespin–Digital Communications GmbH
art director	Tino Schmidt
designer	Tino Schmidt
client	timespin
software/hardware	Macromedia Freehand, Mac
paper/materials	Conqueror CX22
printing	Offset, stamping

4

design firm	Riordon Design
art director	Dan Wheaton
designer	Alan Krpan
client	The Studio Hair Design & Spa
software/hardware	QuarkXPress
paper/materials	Fraser Pegasus brilliant white 110 lb. cover
printing	CJ Graphics

YOUR NEXT APPOINTMENT IS ON

AT _____

WITH _____

PLEASE CALL 24 HOURS AHEAD OF TIME IF YOU NEED TO CANCEL AN APPOINTMENT

THE STUDIO
HAIR DESIGN + SPA

905 631 0809 TEL   795 BRANT STREET, BURLINGTON, ON L7R 2J3
     570 0347 FAX

4

1

design firm	Zigzag Design
art director	Rachel Karaca
designer	Rachel Karaca
client	Zigzag Design
software/hardware	Adobe Illustrator
paper/materials	Recycled chipboard posters
printing	Letterpress and digital

2	
design firm	Octavo Design
art director	Gary Domoney
client	Physical Best
software/hardware	Adobe Illustrator, Mac
paper/materials	White A artboard 360 gsm
printing	1 PMS plus matte gold foil stamp

3	
design firm	Marius Fahrner Design
art director	Marius Fahrner
designers	Marius Fahrner, David Winderman
client	Fork Unstable Media
software/hardware	Macromedia Freehand
paper/materials	Gmund-Colors 250 gsm
printing	3-color offset

Lisa Westlake
Physiotherapist
Australia Fitness Leader
of the year 1999/2000

Physical Best Pty Ltd
PO Box 116 Central Park
Victoria 3145 Australia
Telephone: 03 9576 2556
Mobile: 0413 804 647
Facsimile: 03 9576 2556
lisa@physicalbest.com
www.physicalbest.com

2

Physical**Best**

DESIGNER

>> HAMBURG >> NEW YORK >> BERLIN

O1

CRYSTAL

3

HH :::: FORK UNSTABLE MEDIA NY HH B ||

FORK
HAMBURG

MAIL || davydope@fork.de INTERNET || http://www.fork.de
ADDRESS || Juliusstrasse 25 TELEPHONE || +49 (40) 432 948 - 34
D - 22769 Hamburg TELEFAX || +49 (40) 432 948 - 11

MADE IN THE BUNDESREPUBLIK

for you

don durand
director of operations

forsomeonespecial.com

suite 2150 - 1055 west hastings street
vancouver bc canada v6e 2e9
t 604 915.9139 f 604 915.9138
e ddurand@forsomeonespecial.com

1	
design firm	karacters design group
art director	Nancy Wu
assoc. creative director	Matthew Clark
designer	Nancy Wu
client	forsomeonespecial.com
software/hardware	Adobe Illustrator, Mac G4
paper/materials	Mohawk Navajo
printing	3-spot-color lithography

flying dreams are always the most magnificent

flight creative

creative direction
corporate identity
brand development

print & publishing
packaging & promoti
web & multimedia

2

STEVE KELLER *VP, Creative Development*

p: 615.320.1444 f: 615.320.0750 | 1701 Church St., Nashville, TN 37203

w: www.ivgroup.cc e: skeller@ivgroup.cc

Nashville / Los Angeles

	2
design firm	Lewis Communications/Nashville
art director	Robert Froedge
designer	Robert Froedge
client	I.V. Group
software/hardware	Adobe Illustrator, QuarkXPress
paper/materials	Classic Crest solar white
printing	2-color/2-color with die-cut corners

flight creative

lisa nankervis 0408 220 473
studio 14/15 inkerman street st kilda victoria 3182
telephone (03) 9534 4690 facsimile (03) 9593 6029
mail@flightcreative.com.au www.flightcreative.com.au

nage systems
ibition & display
rior environment

	3
design firm	Flight Creative
art director	Lisa Nankervis
designers	Lisa Nankervis, Alex Fregon
illustrator	Alex Fregon
client	Flight Creative
software/hardware	Adobe Illustrator
paper/materials	Raleigh Sumo 300 gsm
printing	BD Graphics

JENNIFER WON, designer
617 653 4647 ÷ jenniwon@inkspot-press.com

street, east boston, massachusetts 02128

1

design firm	Inkspot
designer	Jennifer Won
software/hardware	Adobe Illustrator
printing	Letterpress

letterpress + graphic design

1

JENNIFER WON, designer
617 653 4647 ÷ jenniwon@inkspot-press.com

80 border street, east boston, massachusetts 02128

GALLIA

2

STEFANO ZIMEI CHEF

1525 WASHINGTON STREET
BOSTON, MASSACHUSETTS 02118

617 247 4455 PHONE 617 247 4737 FAX

2	
design firm	Kellydesign, inc
art director	Kelly McMurray
designer	Kristie Downing
client	Gallia
software/hardware	Adobe Illustrator, QuarkXPress
paper/materials	Wausau Royal Silk chamois 80 lb.
printing	3/1 offset

3	
design firm	IE Design
art director	Marcie Carson
designer	Cya Nelson
client	Jennifer Nicholson, Pear 1
software/hardware	Adobe Illustrator, Mac G4
paper/materials	Curious Iridescents cyber gray
printing	3/1, die cut, register emboss

Pearl

1311 B Montana Ave.
Santa Monica, CA 90403
tel 310 576 7116
fax 310 576 7126

3

NOW eLEARNING

MoHAMMED AHMED
Founder / CEO

T/630.933.8608 x150
F/630.933.8609
E/mohamed@nowelearning.com
www.nowelearning.com

1793
BLOOMINGDALE ROAD
GLENDALE HEIGHTS / IL /
60139

1

noweLEARNING
//we empower you//

1

design firm	Tom & John: A Design Collaborative
art directors	Tom Sizu, John Givens
designers	Tom Sizu, John Givens
client	Now-eLearning
software/hardware	Adobe Illustrator, Mac
printing	Offset

2

design firm	WomanDriven
designer	Colleen Carr
client	Barbara Reuer, Ph.D.
software/hardware	Mac
paper/materials	Neenah Classic Columns
printing	Graphics Ink Lithography

THERAPY TOPICS
Bereavement Support
Pain Management
Personal Growth
Program & Staff Development
Relaxation
Stress Management
Team & Community Building

TYPES OF SERVICES
Consultation
Direct Therapy
Keynote & Endnote Presentations
Seminars
Workshops

2

smiles happen

Barbara Reuer, PhD
Founder and Director

Music Therapist–Board Certified

breuer@musicworxofcalifornia.com

12570-73 Carmel Creek Rd.
San Diego, CA 92130-2314

T | 858 | 755-7710
F | 858 | 259-2806

musicworx™

smiles happen

3

design firm	Marius Fahrner Design
art director	Marius Fahrner
designer	Marius Fahrner
illustrator	Marius Fahrner
client	Lia Staehlin Jewelers
software/hardware	Macromedia Freehand
paper/materials	Roemerturm Curtis Esparto 250 gsm
printing	1-color offset plus gold

4

design firm	Gardner Design
designer	Brian Miller
client	John Crowe Photography
software/hardware	Macromedia Freehand
printing	Printmaster, 3 color

Schönhauser Allee 74a   T +49 (0) 30.44 73 10 13
10437 Berlin   17
www.stereobloc.de   F =   12
                         ISDN =

                                        maik@stereobloc.de

Maik Brummundt

stereobloc

1	
design firm	Stereobloc
art director	Udo Albrecht
designer	Maik Brummundt
client	Stereobloc
software/hardware	QuarkXPress
paper/materials	Chromolux
printing	2 color

2	
design firm	Kontrapunkt D.O.O.
art director	Eduard Čehovin
designer	Eduard Čehovin
client	A Atalanta, Slovenia
software/hardware	Adobe Illustrator
printing	Offset

1

2

AATALANTA

Branislav Srdič, producer
Tobačna ulica 12
SI - 1000 Ljubljana, Slovenia
mobile: +386 41 679 500
E-mail: brana@aatalanta.si

T +386 1 28 33 888
F +386 1 28 31 621

A ATALANTA
FILM + VIDEO
PRODUCTION
& SERVICES

069 . **49 93 41**   tel

Heike Hartmann
visuelle kommunikation

3

Birsteiner Strasse 29
D-60386 Frankfurt a. M.
hh.vk@t-online.de

069 . **49 93 41**   tel

069 . 48 00 25 14   fax
069 . 48 00 25 13   isdn

Heike Hartmann
visuelle kommunikation

3	
design firm	Visuelle Kommunikation
art director	Heike Hartmann
client	Visuelle Kommunikation
software/hardware	QuarkXPress, Mac
paper/materials	Munken Lynx Zartweiss, 2405
printing	Offset Druckerei Sauerland GmbH

4	
design firm	Morrow McKenzie Design
designer	Elizabeth Morrow McKenzie
client	Morrow McKenzie Design
software/hardware	QuarkXPress, Adobe Illustrator, Adobe Photoshop
paper/materials	French construction
printing	Offset, 2 hits white

principal principal **ELIZABETH MORROW·MCKENZIE**
elizabeth@morrow·mckenzie.com

MORROW
McKENZIE
TEL 503·222·0331
FAX 503·296·2332
322 NW 5TH AVE SUITE 313
PORTLAND, OREGON 97209

4

1

design firm	Detroit Creative
art director	Sonja Keserich
designer	Sonja Keserich
client	Detroit Creative
software/hardware	Adobe Illustrator, QuarkXPress, Mac
paper/materials	Pegasus
printing	Hemlock Printers

2

design firm	Melissa Bland
art director	Melissa Bland
client	Triple Space Studio
software/hardware	Adobe Illustrator
paper/materials	Mohawk
printing	2-color offset, Alpha Press

terrafirma

Designer Jewelry by Tina Vennegaard

T 818 386 2029   F 818 784 2486   terrafirmajewelry.com

3

3	
design firm	IE Design
art director	Marcie Carson
designer	Marcie Carson
client	Terra Firma Jewelry
software/hardware	Adobe Illustrator, Mac G3
paper/materials	Neenah Classic Columns Duplex
printing	2/1

TELEVISION WITH ALTITUDE

4

4	
design firm	iridium, a design company
art directors	Mario L'Ecuyer, Jean-Luc Denat
designer	Mario L'Ecuyer
illustrators	Mario L'Ecuyer, Etienne Bessette
client	TetherCam Systems
software/hardware	Adobe Illustrator, Adobe Photoshop, QuarkXPress, Mac G3
paper/materials	Mohawk Superfine smooth cover, custom die cut
printing	2 spot colors (blue and gray)

TETHER CAM

TetherCam Systems Inc.

Laura L. Sheft
Director of Sales

Vox 201.934.8950
Pag 888.614.5368

25A Bentley Avenue.Nepean.Ontario.Canada.K2E 6T7

Fax 201.934.8950
E-mail sales@tethercam.com

	1
design firm	iridium, a design company
art directors	Mario L'Ecuyer, Jean-Luc Denat
designer	Mario L'Ecuyer
illustrator	Mario L'Ecuyer
client	CoCreations Lighting Design
software/hardware	Adobe Photoshop, QuarkXPress, Mac G3
paper/materials	Gilbert Gilclear heavy
printing	2/0, 1 spot color (black) plus match metallic ink

	2
design firm	Papercut Interactive, Inc.
art director	Jason Hill
designer	Jason Hill
client	Papercut Interactive, Inc.
software/hardware	Macromedia Freehand
paper/materials	Stainless steel
printing	Chemical etching

1

1

design firm	Firebelly Design Co.
art director	Dawn Hancock
designer	Dawn Hancock
client	Location Hound
software/hardware	Adobe Illustrator, Mac G4
paper/materials	Strathmore
printing	2/2 offset, Ladendorf Bros.

2

design firm	Sayles Graphic Design
art director	John Sayles
designers	John Sayles, Som Inthalangsy
illustrator	John Sayles
client	2001 Iowa State Fair
software/hardware	Adobe Illustrator, QuarkXPress
paper/materials	Mohawk Superfine 100 lb. cover
printing	Offset

where ideas take flight

3

design firm	Rule 29
art directors	Justin Ahrens, Jim Boborci
designers	Justin Ahrens, Jom Borborci, Jon McGrath
client	Ascentives
software/hardware	Adobe Illustrator, QuarkXPress
paper/materials	Neenah Classic Crest Avon brilliant white 100 lb. cover
printing	O'Neil Printing

ascentives™
corporate speciality solutions

702 N Midvale Blvd | Madison, WI 53705
T **608 231 2488** F 608 231 1382
ascentivescss.com

PAUL YATES
Executive Vice President
paul@ascentivescss.com

3

| SEC | ROW | SEAT |
| 215 | 508 | 7730 |

www.allballinc.net
GAME: 07

allball!

161 Leverington Ave
Suite 3001
Philadelphia, PA 19127

215.508.7730 ph
215.508.7732 fax

TOM CURTIS
general manager

tomcurtis@allballinc.net

+1 215 508 7730

| 215 | 508 | 7730 |
| SEC | ROW | SEAT |

4

4

design firm	D4 Creative Group
art director	Wicky Lee
illustrator	Michael Hurley
client	All Ball, Inc.
software/hardware	Adobe Illustrator, QuarkXPress
printing	2 PMS colors

www.allballinc.net
215.508.7730

allball!

camps
competitions
personal training
program development

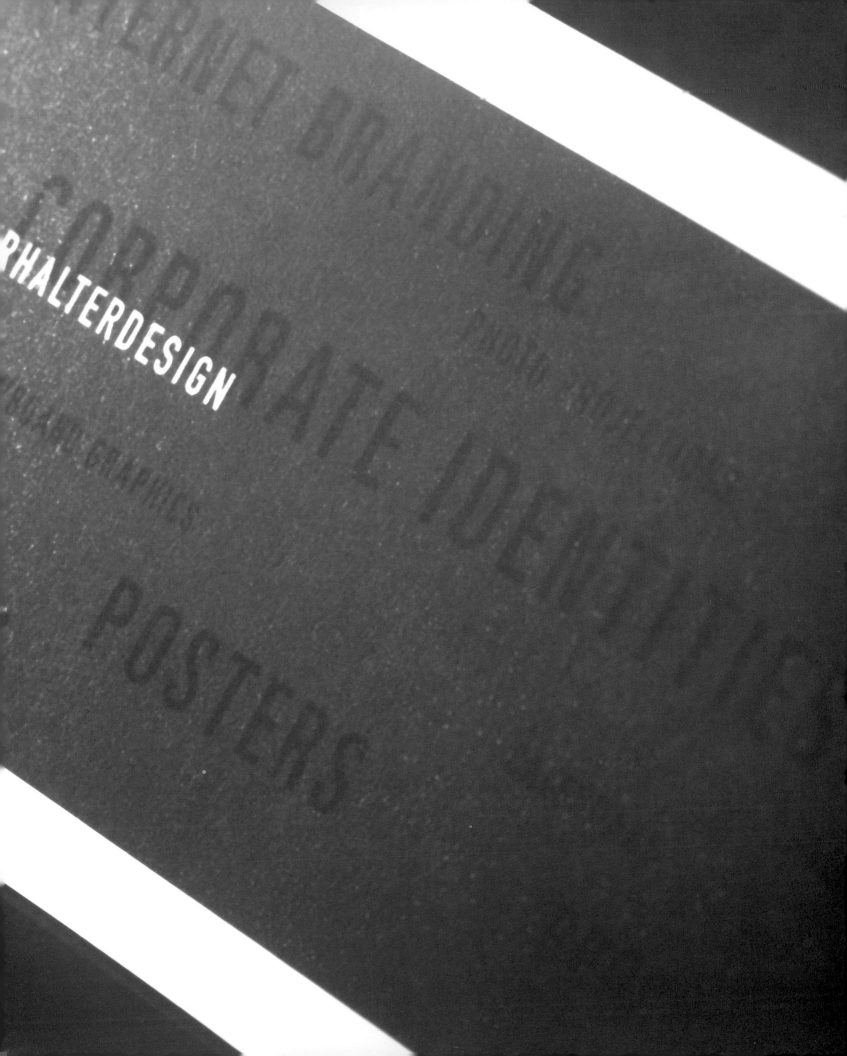

design firm	Geyrhalter Design
art director	Fabian Geyrhalter
designer	Fabian Geyrhalter
client	Geyrhalter Design
software/hardware	Adobe Illustrator, Mac
paper/materials	12 pt. Cornwall C2S, stock, Domtar
printing	4/4, varnish (dull) and metallic

DR. MED. BIRGID PUHL

Fachärztin für Anästhesie, Gesundheitsökonomin (EBS)

Telefon / Fax: 040 - 480 09 17 · Mobil: 0172 - 436 58 80

Klosterstern 5 · D - 20149 Hamburg

mail: BIRGID PUHL@AOL.COM

1

1	
design firm	Marius Fahrner Design
art director	Marius Fahrner
designer	Marius Fahrner
calligrapher	Marius Fahrner
client	Dr. Birgid Puhl
software/hardware	Macromedia Freehand
paper/materials	IGEPA Extra 250 gsm
printing	2-color/2-color offset Pantone

2	
design firm	Up Design Bureau
art director	Chaney Kimball
designer	Chaney Kimball
illustrator	Chaney Kimball
client	Kimball Insurance Agency
software/hardware	Macromedia Freehand
paper/materials	Cougar 100 lb. cover
printing	Velocity Press

NOTES

2

RONALD D. KIMBALL
402 NORTH WASHINGTON
P.O. BOX 723
WELLINGTON, KS 67152

TEL 620.326.7413
FAX 620.326.2548

WEB WWW.KIMBALLINS.COM
EMAIL KIMBALL@SUTV.COM

KIMBALL INSURANCE AGENCY INC

GRAEME LAW & ASSOCIATES | PTY LTD
HIGH STREET EAST KEW
667
VICTORIA AUSTRALIA
3102
TELEPHONE
03 9857 0716
FACSIMILE
03 9819 7629
EMAIL
GLA@GLAP.COM.AU

3

ARCHITECTS GLA

3

design firm	Octavo Design
art director	Gary Domoney
client	Graeme Law & Associates, Architects
software/hardware	Adobe Illustrator, Mac
paper/materials	Saxton Smooth 300 gsm
printing	2 PMS colors on front, 3 PMS colors on back

4

design firm	Williams and House
art dircotor	Pam Williams
designer	Fred Schaub
client	The Artcraft Company
software/hardware	Adobe Illustrator, QuarkXPress, Mac
paper/materials	Crane's 100% cotton, fluorescent white, wove 110 lb. cover
printing	The Artcraft Company; engraving, blind embossing, lithography

the artcraft company

john dumouchel, president

238 john dietsch boulevard
north attleboro, ma 02760
T (800) 659 4042 F (508) 699 6769
john@artcraft.com artcraft.com

4

1

design firm	Anastasia Design
art director	Anastasia Tanis
designer	Bryan Durning
client	Grazioso Pictures, Inc.
software/hardware	QuarkXPress
paper/materials	Strathmore
printing	Lithocraft

2

design firm	Duck Soup Graphics, Inc.
art director	Bill Doucette
designer	Bill Doucette
client	Independent Wholesale
software/hardware	Adobe Illustrator
paper/materials	Speckletone
printing	3 color

ASIA**AROUND**

asiaaround@compuserve.de

YANG-SOON KANG

Susannenstraße 13   20357 Hamburg   G...

Telefon ++49-40-43 05 451   Telefax ++49-

3

WWW.ASIAAROUND.COM

ASIA**AROUND**
HAMBURG

LEBENSMITTEL · ACCESOIRES · GESCHENKE · KÜCHENARTIKEL

design firm	Marius Fahrner Design
art director	Marius Fahrner
designer	Marius Fahrner
illustrator	Marius Fahrner
client	Asia Around
software/hardware	Macromedia Freehand
printing	2 color, Pantone uncoated, offset

4

design firm	Hambly & Woolley, Inc.
art directors	Bob Hambly, Barb Woolley
designer	Gord Woolley
client	In2 Design Solutions Inc.
software/hardware	QuarkXPress, Mac
printing	2/2 registered emboss

In2 Design Solutions Inc.
www.in2-design.com

in2design

419 Jevlan Drive, Unit 1
Vaughan, Ontario L4L 8A9

T: 905.265.8336
F: 905.265.8943

4

Norbert Glahn

Am Böckenbusch 20
51429 Bergisch Gladbach
Tel. +49 . 22 04 . 7 40 44
Fax +49 . 22 04 . 7 40 45
nglahn@ahg.de

1

design firm	graphische formgebung
art director	Herbert Rohsiepe
designer	Herbert Rohsiepe
client	Norbert & Sonja Glahn
software/hardware	Macromedia Freehand, Mac
paper/materials	Roemerturm Precioso
printing	One color (gray), embossing

2

design firm	Little Spoons, Inc.
art director	Christine Moog
designer	Christine Moog
client	Little Spoons, Inc.
software/hardware	QuarkXPress, Mac
paper/materials	Uncoated, small trim
printing	1 color, 2 sided offset

30 FIFTH AVE SUITE 15G
NEW YORK NY 10011
PH 646.644.2008
FAX 212.614.6952
MURPHY@NYC.RR.COM

CHRISTINE N. MOOG
LITTLE SPOONS, INC.

3

design firm	re: salzman designs
art director	Ida Cheinman
designers	Ida Cheinman, Rick Salzman
client	inSource Solutions
software/hardware	Adobe Illustrator, Mac
paper/materials	Mohawk Navajo 100 lb. double-thick cover
printing	3-color offset, 2-sided, die-cut; London Litho

4

design firm	Design Alchemy
designer	Ole Sørensen
illustrator	Ole Sørensen
client	Delight Hamilton Gallery
software/hardware	Adobe Photoshop, Macromedia Freehand, Mac G4
paper/materials	Microlaminated 12 pt. coated stock
printing	Pr1nt.com

ins◊urce

Barbara I. Friedland
Director of Sales

p 410 342 3130 x. 225
e bif@insourcesolutions.com

3

INSOURCE SOLUTIONS

913 S. Lakewood Avenue
Baltimore, Md 21224
1 877 610 5974 f 410 342 6341
www.insourcesolutions.com

dabi@delighthamiltongallery.com
157 So. Jackson, Seattle WA 98104   206.223.9446

dg DELIGHT
HAMILTON
GALLERY

dabi stathakopo

www.delighthamiltongallery.com

4

Gouthier Design
Jonathan J Gouthier

2604 NORTHWEST 54 STREET   PH 954 739 7430   JON@GOUTHIER.COM
FORT LAUDERDALE, FL 33309   FX 954 739 3746   WWW.GOUTHIER.COM

1

	1
design firm	Gouthier Design Inc.
art director	Jonathan Gouthier
designers	Kiley Del Valle, Jonathan Gouthier
client	Gouthier Design, Inc.
software/hardware	QuarkXPress, Mac G3
paper/materials	Mohawk Superfine 110 lb. cover
printing	Blind emboss, match green, engraving, offset match gray, offset match green, and cream

	2
design firm	Monster Design
art directors	Hannah Wygal, Theresa Monica
client	Owen Roberts Group
software/hardware	Macromedia Freehand, Mac
paper/materials	Mohawk Superfine 80 lb. cover
printing	The Press

2

OWEN ROBERTS GROUP

Will Harrison Controller/Accountant
willh@owenrobertsgroup.com

V 425.483.0234
F 425.481.0299
22121 17th Ave SE, bldg E-108
Bothell, Washington 98021

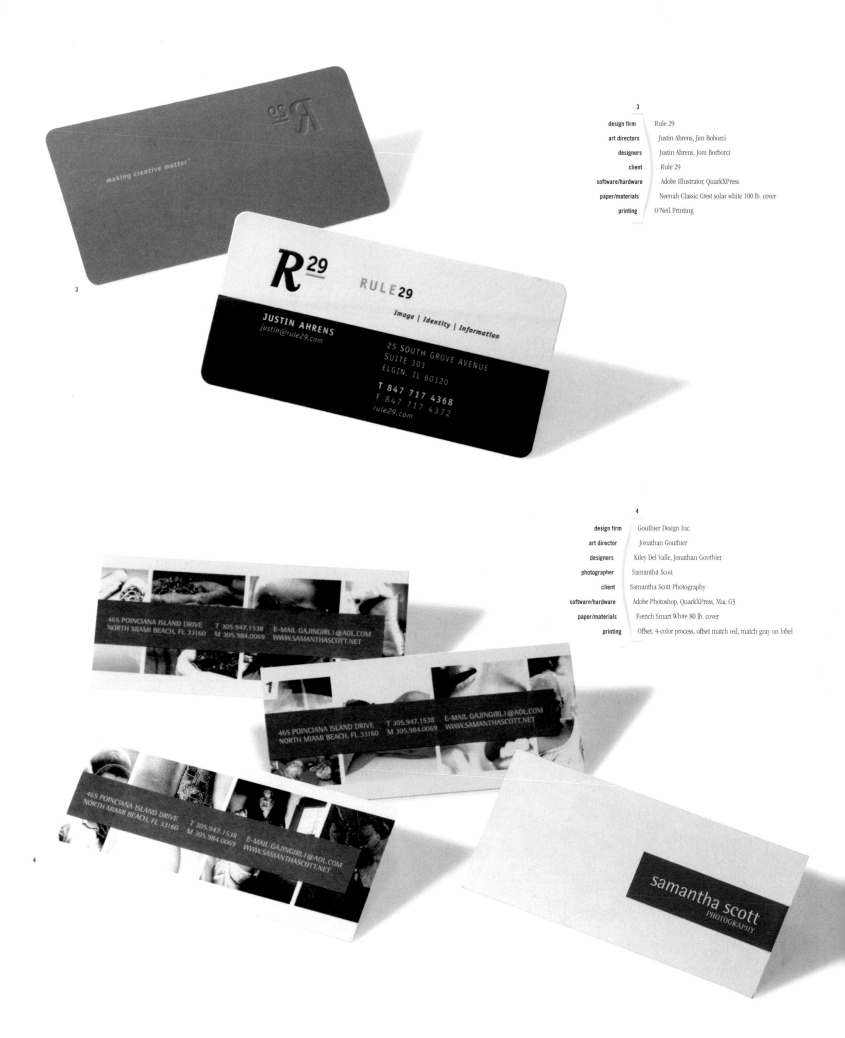

3

design firm	Rule 29
art directors	Justin Ahrens, Jim Boborci
designers	Justin Ahrens, Jom Borborci
client	Rule 29
software/hardware	Adobe Illustrator, QuarkXPress
paper/materials	Neenah Classic Crest solar white 100 lb. cover
printing	O'Neil Printing

making creative matter™

3

R²⁹   RULE 29

Image | Identity | Information

JUSTIN AHRENS
justin@rule29.com

25 SOUTH GROVE AVENUE
SUITE 301
ELGIN, IL 60120

T 847 717 4368
F 847 717 4372
rule29.com

4

design firm	Gouthier Design Inc.
art director	Jonathan Gouthier
designers	Kiley Del Valle, Jonathan Gouthier
photographer	Samantha Scott
client	Samantha Scott Photography
software/hardware	Adobe Photoshop, QuarkXPress, Mac G3
paper/materials	French Smart White 80 lb. cover
printing	Offset, 4-color process, offset match red, match gray on label

4

465 POINCIANA ISLAND DRIVE   T 305.947.1538   E-MAIL GAJINGIRL1@AOL.COM
NORTH MIAMI BEACH, FL 33160   M 305.984.0069   WWW.SAMANTHASCOTT.NET

465 POINCIANA ISLAND DRIVE   T 305.947.1538   E-MAIL GAJINGIRL1@AOL.COM
NORTH MIAMI BEACH, FL 33160   M 305.984.0069   WWW.SAMANTHASCOTT.NET

465 POINCIANA ISLAND DRIVE   T 305.947.1538   E-MAIL GAJINGIRL1@AOL.COM
NORTH MIAMI BEACH, FL 33160   M 305.984.0069   WWW.SAMANTHASCOTT.NET

samantha scott
PHOTOGRAPHY

design firm	Oakley Design Studios
art director	Tim Oakley
designer	Tim Oakley
illustrator	Tim Oakley
client	Vista Continental
software/hardware	Adobe Illustrator
paper/materials	Beckett Ridge Cameo
printing	Mollet Printing, 1 color with foil stamps

VISTA CONTINENTAL

HERSCHEL ADWELL III
Vice President / Operations

~ SIR WILLIAM'S COURT ~
851 South Rampart Boulevard
Suite 150
Las Vegas, Nevada 89128
Office: 702.228.2077
Fax: 702.228.1837
Cell: 702.610.5363
e-mail: adwell@vistacontinental.com

VISTA CONTINENTAL
·CORPORATION·

HERSCHEL ADWELL III
Vice President/Operations

M3 ADVERTISING DESIGN
meaning + message + mystery

M³

ads) annual reports) brochures) campaigns
copywriting (design identity) illustration
interactive) packaging) print) web

Dan McElhattan III
dan@m3ad.com

M³

3230 W. Flamingo Road Suite 8 Las Vegas Nevada 89121

www.m3ad.com

702 796 6323 Tel
893 6323 Fax

1

1	
design firm	M3AD.com
art director	Dan McElhattan III
designer	Dan McElhattan III
client	M3 Advertising Design
software/hardware	Adobe Illustrator
paper/materials	Neenah solar white 100 lb. cover
printing	R+S Printing, 2/1 color

2	
design firm	Kolegram Design
art director	Mike Teixeira
designer	Gontran Blais
client	Kolegram Design
software/hardware	Adobe Illustrator, QuarkXPress
paper/materials	Strathmore Grandee and Sticker
printing	Du Progrès

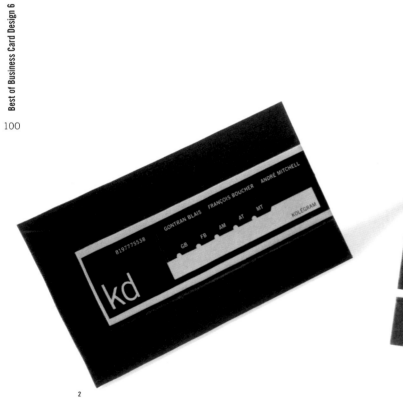

GONTRAN BLAIS   FRANÇOIS BOUCHER   ANDRÉ MITCHELL
8197775538   GB   FB   AM   AT   MT   KOLEGRAM

kd

WWW.KOLEGRAM.COM
ANNIE TANGUAY   MIKE TEIXEIRA

designartstyle   K

ANNIE TANGUAY   MIKE TEIXEIRA

designartstyle   WWW.KOLEGRAM.COM   K

2

:: CODE RED DESIGN

RENÉE SALLEE

GRAPHIC DESIGNER

TEL 818.634.9908
FAX 818.885.7669
RENEE@CODERED-DESIGN.COM
WWW.CODERED-DESIGN.COM

3

design firm	Code Red Design
art director	Renée Sallee
designer	Renée Sallee
illustrator	Renée Sallee
client	Code Red Design, Renée Sallee
software/hardware	Adobe Illustrator, PC
paper/materials	Mead dull-coated cover, white
printing	4/3, metallic ink and die cut, Hayes & Company Printing, Inc.

4

anna midori abe
photography

tel 425 702 9646
mobile 206 975 7376

5524 157th drive north east
redmond, wa 98052

design firm	Monster Design
art directors	Hannah Wygal, Theresa Monica
client	Anna Midori Abe Photography
software/hardware	Macromedia Freehand, Mac
paper/materials	Mohawk Superfine 80 lb. cover
printing	The Press

1

2

1	
design firm	Function
designer	Jeff Culver
client	Exem Company
software/hardware	QuarkXPress
paper/materials	Classic Crest

2	
design firm	Campbell Fisher Design
art director	Ken Peters
designer	Ken Peters
illustrator	Ken Peters
client	Rhino Sports
software/hardware	Adobe Illustrator, Mac G4
paper/materials	Classic Crest 130 lb. cover
printing	3/3 offset

3

design firm	Brainforest, Inc.
art director	Nils Bunde
designer	Adam Moroschan
client	The Northridge Group
software/hardware	Adobe Illustrator, QuarkXPress
paper/materials	Mohawk Superfine
printing	Lake County Press

3

Therese K. Fauerbach
Chief Executive Officer
Tel 847 692.6720
Fax 847 518.2263

The Northridge Group, Inc.

9700 W. Higgins Road Suite 690
Rosemont, IL 60018-4710

www.northridgegroup.com
therese.fauerbach@northridgegroup.com

EYEMATIC

larry mcDonough
senior director product
management, authoring tools

1085 mission street
san francisco, ca 94103

phone (415) 335-4751
cell (408) 375-2831
fax (415) 575-4756

www.eyematic.com
larry.mcdonough@eyematic.com

1

	1
design firm	Gateway Arts
art director	Dave Carlson
designer	Gina Cusano
client	Eyematic
software/hardware	Adobe Illustrator
paper/materials	100 lb. cover
printing	3/1, die cut

	2
design firm	Artministry, Inc.
art director	John O'Brien
designer	John O'Brien
client	Artministry, Inc.
software/hardware	Adobe Illustrator, QuarkXPress, Mac
paper/materials	Chromecoat
printing	2/1 PMS, G-2 Graphics

WWW.ARTMINISTRY.COM

JOHN O'BRIEN
PRESIDENT / CREATIVE DIRECTOR
JOHN@ARTMINISTRY.COM

ARTMINISTRY, INC
5211 KESTER AVE SUITE 201 SHERMAN OAKS CA 91411
T 818 995 6597 **F** 818 995 4599 **WWW.ARTMINISTRY.COM**

2

David Giles
MANAGER, NATIONAL HOME IMPROVEMENT SALES

579 Richmond Street West, Suite 100
Toronto, Ontario MSV 1Y6

T 416-364-8741 EXT. 105
F 416-367-4242
C 647-284-2227
E dgiles@gtwcanada.com

3

GEORGETOWN
PUBLICATIONS

3

design firm	Mindwalk Design Group, Inc.
art director	Michael Huggins, RGD
designer	Oliver Sutherns
client	Georgetown Publications
software/hardware	Adobe Illustrator, Macromedia Freehand, QuarkXPress
paper/materials	Classic Crest solar white 80 lb. cover
printing	Halton Commercial Printers

4

design firm	Burgeff Co.
art director	Patrick Burgeff
illustrator	Patrick Burgeff
client	Laura Gómez, Guia de Diseño Mexicano
software/hardware	Macromedia Freehand
paper/materials	Opalina paper
printing	Silkscreen

laucet@mexicandesign.com

Guía de Diseño Mexicano

Laura C. Gómez, Directora

(55)8500 1086
(55)5554 5931
(55)8500 1112 (DF)

4

www.mexicandesign.com
GUÍADEDISEÑO
mexicano

NEXT APPOINTMENT

NO 682-7037

Time: _____ Date: _____

Christy Peters

CHEZ BELLE SALON
535 N. Woodlawn, Ste. 345
Cellular Phone: 841-1692

NO 682-7323

style

Jill Corey Vartenigian
13546 36th Ave NE
Seattle, WA 98125

206.418.0984

MOMENTUM PRESS AND DESIGN
206.418.0984

1

design firm	Up Design Bureau
art director	Travis Brown
designer	Travis Brown
client	Christy Peters
software/hardware	Macromedia Freehand, Mac G4
paper/materials	Luna 100 lb. cover
printing	Velocity Press

2

design firm	Momentum Press and Design
art director	Jill Vartenigian
designer	Jill Vartenigian
client	Momentum Press and Design
paper/materials	Rives BFK; handset lead type and dingbat
printing	Letterpress; Chandler and Price Letterpress

Level I/157 Franklin Street Adelaide SA
PO Box 6687 Halifax Street Adelaide SA 5000

08 8211 7200

e peter@pandaca.biz f 08 8211 9800

3

3
design firm	Voice
art director	Scott Carslake
designer	Anthony De Leo
client	P@A Chartered Accountants
software/hardware	Macromedia Freehand
paper/materials	Saxton
printing	Finsbury Press

P&a
Andrew Y F Wong *Partner*
Chartered Accountants & Business Advisers

4
design firm	Campbell Fisher Design
art directors	Greg Fisher, Ken Peters
designer	Ken Peters
client	Estilo Boutique
software/hardware	Adobe Illustrator, Mac G4
paper/materials	Domtar Solutions 120 lb. cover
printing	2/2 offset

ESTĪLO

4

Kelly Dixon
Owner

6735 East Greenway Parkway
Suite 1050
Scottsdale, Arizona 85254

Direct: (917) 847-6633
Fax: (480) 634-8828

estiloboutique@hotmail.com

801 South Dallas Street, Baltimore MD 21231
phone 410.563.4038 fax 410.732.0601
email mackerel@mindspring.com

Maureen T Haines, AIA
Principal

1

mackerel sky Architecture

1	
design firm	Blank, Inc.
art director	Robert Kent Wilson
designer	Robert Kent Wilson
client	Mackerel Sky Architecture
software/hardware	Adobe Illustrator, Mac G4
paper/materials	Starwhite 80 lb. cover
printing	G+F Printing

Ana Paola Villegas [office]
310 766 3916 [phone]   ana@splicehere.com [email]

2

splicehere
editorial

2	
design firm	Bluespark Studios
art director	David Brzozowski
designer	David Brzozowski
illustrator	David Brzozowski
client	Splice Here Editorial
software/hardware	Adobe Illustrator, Adobe Photoshop
paper/materials	Classic Crest
printing	3/1

3

design firm	Untitled
art directors	David Hawkins, Glenn Howard
client	Karena Batstone
paper/materials	G. F. Smith Dutch unlined grayboard
printing	2-color lithography

Karena Batstone Design

Call 0117 944 1004
Fax 0117 944 1153
Mail info@karenabatstone.com
View www.karenabatstone.com
Post 21 Somerset Street, Kingsdown, Bristol BS2 8LZ

design firm	Marius Fahrner Design
art director	Marius Fahrner
designer	Marius Fahrner
illustrator	Marius Fahrner
client	My Mother
software/hardware	Macromedia Freehand
paper/materials	Design Offset, IGEPA, 250 gsm
printing	2-color offset, Pantone

2

design firm	Visual Dialogue & Rick Rawlins
art directors	Fritz Klaetke, Rick Rawlins
designers	Rick Rawlins, Fritz Klaetke, Ian Varrassi
client	Agent
software/hardware	QuarkXPress, Mac G4
paper/materials	White plastic with magnetic strip
printing	Step Direct

1

IRENE FAHRNER

Schillerstrasse 38 | D-86161 Augsburg | Telefon: +49 (0) 821-55 32 03

2

EDANA SPICKER 001@AGENTEDANA.COM

617 522 3363

AGENT

3

Luis Albuquerque **PHOTOGRAPHER**

233 Carlaw Avenue, No. 408, Toronto ON M4M 3N6   T 416 461 2766 F 416 461 4797

ALBUQUERQUE

3	
design firm	Hambly & Woolley, Inc.
art directors	Bob Hambly, Barb Woolley
designer	Emese Ungar
client	Luis Albuquerque, Photographer
software/hardware	QuarkXPress, Mac
printing	2/1 Lithography

4	
design firm	Gardner Design
art director	Bill Gardner
client	Windowsill Foods
software/hardware	Macromedia Freehand
printing	Printmaster, 2 color

{ POST OFFICE BOX # 1595 }
{ LAWRENCE KANSAS 66044 }
{ UNITED STATES of AMERICA }

WIND WSILL
FOODS

TELEPHONE { 785 838 3800
FACSIMILE { 785 838 4588

*www.*WINDOWSILLFOODS.com

4

oceanmore

oceanmore

urednica
Gordana Farkaš Sfeci

Naklada OceanMore
Vladimira Ruždjaka 37
10 000 Zagreb
tel/fax: 01 604 35 38
e-mail: info@oceanmore.hr
www.oceanmore.hr
————
e-mail: gordana@oceanmore.hr
gsm: 091 503 9765

design firm	Cavarpayer
art director	Cavarpayer
designers	Ira Payer, Lana Cavar
client	Ocean More Publishing
software/hardware	QuarkXPress, Mac G4
paper/materials	Munken Lynx
printing	Offset

Kolēgramdesign

Ⓚ

37, BOULEVARD ST-JOSEPH, HULL (QUÉBEC) J8Y 3V8

819.777.5538 WWW.KOLEGRAM.COM FAX 819.777.8525

	1
design firm	Kolegram Design
art director	Mike Teixeira
designer	Mike Teixeira
client	Kolegram Design
software/hardware	QuarkXPress
paper/materials	Mohawk Navajo
printing	Du Progrès

	2
design firm	Tesser
art directors	(CO) Tre Musco, (AD) Kimberly Cross
designer	Sandrine Albouy
client	Tesser
software/hardware	Adobe Illustrator, Mac G4
paper/materials	10 pt. Alameda vinyl
printing	Infinity Press

TESSER™

www.tesser.com

Tré Musco
CEO & Chief Creative Officer
415.541.9999

650 Delancey Street, Loft #404
San Francisco, CA 94107
c> 415.672.1683
t> 800.310.4400
f> 415.541.9699
e> tre.musco@tesser.com

Jeremy D. Wunsch
President/Forensic Analyst
jwunsch@lucidatallc.com

PO Box 62182
Minneapolis, MN 55426
612.384.7538
fax 530.732.9218
www.lucidatallc.com

3

design firm	OrangeSeed Design
art director	Damien Wolf
designers	Dale Mustful, Rebecca Miles
client	LuciData
software/hardware	Adobe Illustrator, QuarkXPress, Mac G4
paper/materials	Cougar Opaque 100 lb cover
printing	Customgraphix

4

design firm	Move Creative
art director	Perry Chua
designer	Perry Chua
client	streetdreamz.ca
software/hardware	Adobe Illustrator, Mac G3
paper/materials	McCoy 130 lb. cover
printing	GM Freelance

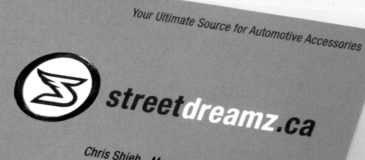

Your Ultimate Source for Automotive Accessories

streetdreamz.ca

Chris Shieh   Managing Director

chrisshieh@streetdreamz.ca
Mobile: 604.649.2016   Fax: 604.946.8457

1

design firm	Prank Design
art director	Michael Crigler
designer	Michael Crigler
illustrator	Michael Crigler
client	Prank Design
software/hardware	Adobe Illustrator
paper/materials	Chipboard, sticker paper

2

design firm	Goodesign
designer	Diane Shaw
client	Lake
software/hardware	QuarkXPress
paper/materials	Starwhite Tiara double-thick cover

jng communications

jennifer gottlieb
246 brattle st #31
cambridge, ma 02138
jgottlieb@jngcommunications.com
617.354.9784 t
617.354.6259 f

3

home collection

4

Annabelle

Jo Ann Silverman
24 Hillside Avenue, Short Hills, NJ 07078
phone 973 376 5733 *fax* 973 564 9258
email annabellehome@aol.com

	3
design firm	Kinetik
art directors	Beth Clawson, Jeff Fabian, Beverley Hunter
designers	Mike Joosse, Natalie Politts, Katie Ratsch, Scott Rier, Katie Roland, Sam Shelton, Jenny Skillman
client	JNG Communications
software/hardware	QuarkXPress, Mac
paper/materials	Smart
printing	Offset

	4
design firm	Goodesign
designer	Kathryn Hammill
client	Annabelle Home
software/hardware	Adobe Illustrator

Jeremy Sun Ting Kung
Senior Manager

orcades:gn

Orcadesign Consultants
7 Purvis Street
Unit 04-01
Singapore 188586
T. +65 6562 3831
F. +65 6562 3603
M. +65 9782 7017
E. jeremy.sun@orcadesign.com.my

孫鼎光

Johor Bahru
56 Jalan Impian Emas 4
Taman Impian Emas
81300 Skudai, Johor
Malaysia
T. +607 558 3380
F. +607 558 3180

A HPI Group Company

1

email nnassar@shore.net

Nassar Design   560 Harrison Avenue Boston MA 02118 482.1464/426.3604

Nélida Nassar

2

1	
design firm	Duffy Singapore
art director	Christopher Lee
designer	Cara Ang
client	Orcadesign Consultants
software/hardware	Macromedia Freehand
paper/materials	Matte art card 360 gsm
printing	2 color, 1 color, matte laminate both sides, die cut

2	
design firm	Nassar Design
art director	Nélida Nassar
designer	Nélida Nassar
client	Nassar Design
software/hardware	QuarkXPress
paper/materials	Ivoline High Speed white 300 gsm
printing	Alpha Press

Mary Jane's Salon

a John Paul Mitchell Systems Signature Salon

3

appointment

for _____

with _____

                            date   time

1630 mineral spring ave., north providence, ri 02904, 401.231.4145

mary jane's salon

cheryl sennett
stylist

1630 mineral spring ave.
north providence
rhode island 02904
401.231.4145

3

design firm	Mirage Design
art director	Mark DaPonte
designer	Lynette Allaire
client	Mary Jane's Salon
software/hardware	Macromedia Freehand
printing	Barrigton Printing

4

design firm	Matter
art director	Rick Griffith
designer	Jennifer Fujimoto
client	Magic Circle Mime Company
software/hardware	Adobe Illustrator, Adobe Photoshop, QuarkXPress
printing	2-color offset, blind embossing

4

DOUGLAS MACINTYRE
3221 35TH AVE, SOUTH SEATTLE, WA 98144 USA
TELEPHONE 206 722 4245
FACSIMILE 206 722 4138
E-MAIL MAGICCIRCL@AOL.COM

MAGIC CIRCLE MIME COMPANY

MAGGIE PETERSEN
67 SANDY LANE WALNUT CREEK, CA 94596 USA
TELEPHONE 925 932 8552
FACSIMILE 925 944 7057
E-MAIL MAGICCIRCLE@AOL.COM

	1	
design firm	Marius Fahrner Design
art director	Marius Fahrner
designer	Marius Fahrner
illustrator	Marius Fahrner
client	Belvedere Real Estate and Consulting
software/hardware	Macromedia Freehand
paper/materials	IGEPA Design offset 250 gsm
printing	2-color, 1-color Pantone

	2	
design firm	Baumann & Baumann
art director	Barbara and Gerd Baumann
designer	Barbara and Gerd Baumann
illustrator	Barbara and Gerd Baumann
client	Baumann & Baumann
software/hardware	Macromedia Freehand
paper/materials	Conqueror Smooth
printing	Offset

Harvey Appelbaum
Creative Director
happel@inc-3.com
www.inc-3.com
220 East 23rd Street   New York, NY 10010   P 212.213.1130   F 212.532.8022

3

	3
design firm	Inc-3
art director	Harvey Appelbaum
designers	Harvey Appelbaum, John Sexton
client	Inc-3
software/hardware	Adobe Illustrator, QuarkXPress
paper/materials	Strathmore Writing
printing	Offset

	4
design firm	91nueveuno
art directors & designers	Carlos Jimeno Gonzáles, Alicia Martínez Diaz
client	91nueveuno
software/hardware	Adobe Illustrator, Mac G3
paper/materials	Business card: white opale polystyrene 0.5 mm
	Label: self-adhesive Avery glossart crack-back plus 85 gsm
printing	Business card: screenprinting, silver color
	Label: offset, 2 match color plus matte varnish

4

Telefon 0711 54 11 12
Telefax 0711 56 07 64

4a

Matthias Burkart
Architektenbüro 4a
Hallstraße 25
70376 Stuttgart

Ernst Ulrich Tillmanns
Architektenbüro 4a
Hallstraße 25
70376 Stuttgart

4a

Telefon 0711 54 11 12
Telefax 0711 56 07 64

Alexander v Salmuth
Architektenbüro 4a
Hallstraße 25
70376 Stuttgart

4a

Telefon 0711 54 11 12
Telefax 0711 56 07 64

Telefon 0711 54 11 12
Telefax 0711 56 07 64

4a

Eberhard Pritzer
Architektenbüro 4a
Hallstraße 25
70376 Stuttgart

1

1

design firm	Baumann & Baumann
art director	Barbara and Gerd Baumann
designer	Barbara and Gerd Baumann
illustrator	Barbara and Gerd Baumann
client	Architektenbüro 4a
software/hardware	Macromedia Freehand
paper/materials	Elfenbeinkarton 246 gsm weiß, glatt
printing	Offset

TOPIC 101

SUSAN BATTISTA SUSAN@TOPIC101.COM
FOUR CONCORD SQUARE BOSTON, MASS 02118
TELEPHONE 617.450.0614

WWW.TOPIC101.COM

2

design firm	Visual Dialogue
art director	Fritz Klaetke
designers	Fritz Klaetke, Ian Varrassi
client	Topic 101
software/hardware	Adobe Illustrator, Adobe Photoshop, QuarkXPress, Mac G4
paper/materials	Springhill tag
printing	Stuart Litho

2

Frankfurt AM MAIN

T   0171_15 55 927

Britta Janas
PRODUKTION

design firm	Simon & Goetz Design
art director	Bernd Vollmoeller
designer	Bernd Vollmoeller
client	Britta Janas, Production
software/hardware	Macromedia Freehand, Mac
paper/materials	Curious Touch, Arjo Wiggins
printing	Offset, silkscreen, hot foil stamp

design firm	Simon & Goetz Design
designer	Bernd Vollmoeller
client	Soles Genus, Balance Care
software/hardware	Macromedia Freehand, Mac
paper/materials	Ikono matte
printing	Offset

1

1

2

design firm	Gardner Design
art directors	Bill Gardner, Brian Miller
client	Shelton Collision Repair
software/hardware	Macromedia Freehand
printing	Printmaster, 3 color, embossing

2

3

Chaitanya (Chet) Kanojia
Chief Technical Officer

275 grove street, newton, ma 02466

617 614 1000 [tel]
617 614 1080 [direct]
617 614 1190 [fax]
ckanojia@navic.tv

www.navic.tv

NAVIC
networks

3	
design firm	Debenham Design, Inc.
art director	Eileen Debenham
designer	Yuko Inagaki
client	Navic Networks
software/hardware	Adobe Illustrator
paper/materials	Starwhite Vicksburg 110 lb. cover
printing	United Lithographics

4	
design firm	Kasuba Design Company
art director	Terri Fry Kasuba
designer	Terri Fry Kasuba
client	Inside & Outside
software/hardware	Adobe Illustrator, Mac
paper/materials	Cougar cover white 100 lb.
printing	Offset

4

INSIDE &
OUTSIDE
your style. your home.

✿

29 West Lancaster Ave.
Ardmore, PA 19003

☎

610.642.8988

....

Carrie McNamara

ROBERT PALMER // design
http://www.rp-network.com/
robertpalmer@mac.com

1

design firm	Robert Palmer Design
designer	Robert Palmer
client	Robert Palmer Design
software/hardware	Adobe Illustrator
paper/materials	Yupo 100 lb. cover
printing	Rush Press

2

design firm	plus design, inc.
art director	Anita Meyer
designers	Anita Meyer, Jan Baker
client	Anago
paper/materials	Mohawk Superfine white smooth 70 lb. text
printing	Alpha Press (foil stamping), McEmbossing, Inc.

a
anago
65 exeter at boylston
boston massachusetts 02116
617.266.6222
fax 617.266.0175

coffeebar
Daniel Wayne & Felicia Ruiz-Wayne
Owners
4404 N. Central Ave. Nº 1, Phoenix AZ 85012
Tel 602.266.6466

3

10 purchased espresso drinks = 1 gratis

3	
design firm	Design Alchemy
designer	Ole Sørensen
illustrator	Ole Sørensen
client	Delight Hamilton Gallery
software/hardware	Adobe Photoshop, Macromedia Freehand, Mac G4
paper/materials	Microlaminated 12 pt. coated stock
printing	Pr1nt.com

4	
design firm	Untitled
art directors	David Hawkins, Glenn Howard
client	Untitled
paper/materials	G. F. Smith Colorplan ebony, Carbon Free
printing	Screenprinted white and yellow

Untitled
Glenn Howard
glenn@untitledstudio.com

4

Untitled
Studio 6
The Lux Building
2/4 Hoxton Square
London N1 6NU
Call 020 7613 3129
Fax 020 7684 6525
www.untitledstudio.com

CONSULTING

N2

NADINE NASSAR
N2_consulting@yahoo.com

MARKETING STRATEGY . VISUAL DESIGN
231 West 26th Street Suite 6 New York NY 10001 T 917 992.8376

1

	1
design firm	Nassar Design
art director	Nélida Nassar
designer	Margarita Encomienda
client	N2 Consulting
software/hardware	QuarkXPress
paper/materials	Mohawk Superfine 100 lb.
printing	Alpha Press

	2
design firm	Rule 29
art director	Justin Ahrens
designers	Justin Ahrens, Jon McGrath
client	Econergy Solutions
software/hardware	Adobe Illustrator, QuarkXPress
paper/materials	Neenah Classic Crest solar white 100 lb. cover

WWW.ECONERGYSOLUTIONS.COM

805 RICHARDS STREET · GENEVA, IL 60134 P 630.881.6890

JASON SCHOEPKE
jason@econergysolutions.com

ECONERGY
SOLUTIONS

2

WWW.DRUZIN.COM

3

RANDI DRUZIN
SPORTS WRITER & EDITOR

RANDI@DRUZIN.COM
WWW.DRUZIN.COM

TELEPHONE:

ADDRESS:

FACSIMILE:

3	
design firm	Red Communications
designer	Curtis Achilles
client	Randi Druzin
software/hardware	Adobe Illustrator
paper/materials	Neenah Classic Crest
printing	2/2, metallic ink

4	
design firm	Up Design Bureau
art director	Chris Parks
designer	Chris Parks
client	Vespa Wichita
software/hardware	Macromedia Freehand, Mac G4
paper/materials	Cougar Cougar 100 lb.
printing	Velocity Press

4

www.vespausa.com

Vespa
kansas city

⊙ Kurt Starks
scooter enthusiast
kurt@vespakansas

⊙ Kurt Starks
scooter enthusiast
kurt@vespawichita.com

Vespa
wichita

511 east douglas avenue
wichita . kansas . 67202
telephone 316 263 9900
facsimile . 316 263 9907
www.vespawichita.com

1	
design firm	Drotz Design
art director	Dallas Drotz
designer	Dallas Drotz
client	Drotz Design
software/hardware	Adobe Illustrator
paper/materials	Sappi Vintage velvet/blank
printing	4-color offset, varnish

2	
design firm	Matter
art director	Rick Griffith
client	Airbubble Industries
software/hardware	Adobe Illustrator, Adobe Photoshop, QuarkXPress
printing	2-color offset

3

design firm	Voice
art director	Anthony De Leo
designer	Anthony De Leo
client	Shorts Film Festival
software/hardware	Macromedia Freehand
paper/materials	Tablex
printing	Douglas Press

4

design firm	Northbank
art director	Simon Cryer
client	Timeslice Films, Ltd.
paper/materials	Mellotex
printing	4-color process

Tim Macmillan
Timeslice Films Limited
Unit 22 Brassmill Enterprise Centre
Brassmill Lane, Bath BA1 3JN
T: +44 (0) 1225 420988
F: +44 (0) 1225 480734
E: timeslicefilms@btinternet.com
www.timeslicefilms.com

PR1NT

T2062193380
C2063513675

VICKI KNAPP·AGENT

WWW.PR1NT.COM
VICKI@PR1NT.COM

PR1NT HEADQUARTERS
№ 921, 1122 E. PIKE ST
SEATTLE, WA. 98122 USA

pr1nt.com is the print brokering division of design alchemy creatis

1

design firm	Design Alchemy
art director	Ole Sørensen
designer	Ole Sørensen
illustrator	Ole Sørensen
client	Pr1nt.com
software/hardware	Macromedia Freehand, Mac G4
paper/materials	12 pt. coated stock
printing	Pr1nt.com, 4/4 with spot metallic silver overprint

2

design firm	Voice
art director	Scott Carslake
designer	Anthony De Leo
client	Lotus
software/hardware	Macromedia Freehand
paper/materials	White A artboard
printing	Embossing, Finsbury Press

chloe papazahariakis

fashion designer
stylist
make-up artistry
event coordination
public relations
wardrobe consultant

32 college road
kent town sa 5067

fon/fax +61 8 8363 3271
mobile 0402 255 729
kloegirl@hotmail.com

lotus

everything loved is the centre of a paradise

STEMCOBIO

Erica Deibert
Scientist
edeibert@stemcobiomedical.com

→ **919.484.2571** x258

2810 Meridian Parkway, Suite 148
Durham, North Carolina 27713

→ **919.484.8792** FAX

3

design firm	Forma Design
art director	David Chapin
designer	Nancy Schruers
client	Stemco Biomedical
software/hardware	Macromedia Freehand, Mac
paper/materials	Fox River Select bright white wove 88 lb.
printing	Americolor, offset

4

design firm	Dan Elliott
designer	Dan Elliott
illustrator	Dan Elliott
client	Dan Elliott
software/hardware	Adobe Illustrator, QuarkXPress, Mac
paper/materials	Matte art board 350 gsm
printing	2 color

Dan Elliott. Graphic Design.
E. DELLIOTT22@HOTMAIL.COM
M. 07876 026 269

LIFE'S {ESSENTIALS}

LIFE'S {ESSENTIALS} le

CLAIRE BUSHELL

2 DILLON ST
BLENHEIM
NEW ZEALAND

T/F: 03 578 7472
M: 021 235 6404
E: lifes.essentials@paradise.net.nz

> CONSULT > COOK > COMPUTE > CREATE >

1

design firm	Lloyds Graphic Design & Communication
art director	Alexander Lloyd
designer	Alexander Lloyd
client	Life's Essentials
software/hardware	Adobe Photoshop, Macromedia Freehand, Mac G4
paper/materials	Matte art board 250 gsm
printing	Offset

2

design firm	Hambly & Woolley, Inc.
art directors	Bob Hambly, Barb Woolley
designer	Dominic Ayre
client	Kohn Architects Inc.
software/hardware	QuarkXPress, Mac
printing	2/1, die cut

Kohn

Kohn Architects

Kohn Architects Inc.
116 Spadina Ave, Suite 501, Toronto ON M5V 2K6
Telephone 416.703.6700 Fax 416.703.6704
www.kohnarchitects.com

Sean Lawrence AA Dip, Senior Associate
slawrence@kohnarchitects.com

2

libby lodge president

thirty things, llc 5 washington avenue suite 5 cambridge ma 02140
telephone/telefax 617.441.3544 email thirtythings@mediaone.net

3

3	
design firm	Nassar Design
art director	Nélida Nassar
designer	Margarita Encomienda
client	Thirty Things
software/hardware	Adobe Illustrator, QuarkXPress
paper/materials	Monadnock Caress Cover smooth mellow white 100 lb.
printing	Alpha Press

4	
design firm	Splash Interactive
art director	Ivy Wong
designer	Ivy Wong
client	Splash Interactive
software/hardware	Adobe Illustrator, Mac G4
paper/materials	Curiosity
printing	Letterpress, die cut

4

beyondbricks
The internet entrepreneurs portal

Beyond Bricks
Sir John Lyon House
5 High Timber Street
Blackfriars
London
EC4V 3NX

T 020 7420 7724
F 020 7420 7701
E info@beyondbricks.com

Neil Howlin
Beyond Bricks
Sir John Lyon House
5 High Timber Street
Blackfriars
London
EC4V 3NX

T 020 7557 4604
F 020 7420 7701
M 0777 578 0608
E neilh@beyondbricks.com

beyondbricks
The internet entrepreneurs portal

www.beyondbricks.com

2

design firm	Wilson Harvey
art director	Paul Burgess
designer	Dan Elliott
client	DTI Beyond Bricks
software/hardware	Adobe Illustrator, QuarkXPress, Mac
paper/materials	Art board 350 gsm
printing	2-color lithography

1

2

design firm	Pure Imagination Studios
art director	Josh Williams
designer	Josh Williams
illustrator	Josh Williams
client	Shining City Records
software/hardware	Macromedia Freehand, Mac
printing	Lithographics Services, Inc.

3

design firm	Kolegram Design
art director	Mike Teixeira
designer	Francois Boucher
client	Vertige Design
software/hardware	QuarkXPress
paper/materials	Cornwall coated 25
printing	Imprimerie Gauvin

SHINING CITY
RECORDS

Titus Heard
Producer

291 S. La Cienega Blvd., #736
Beverly Hills, CA 90211
(310) 365.5453
titus@shiningcity.com

819 568°03'08

FRANCOIS BOUCHER
VERTIGEDESIGN @SYMPATICO.CA
30 RUE DES BRETONS
GATINEAU QUÉBEC J8T 6E8

3

LANE DURANTE
1801 Dove Street, Suite 104
Newport Beach, CA 92653
Ph. 949.261.7857
Fx. 949.261.5966
lane@damionhickman.com
www.damionhickman.com

DAMION HICKMAN DESIGN

DAMION HICKMAN
1801 Dove Street, Suite 104
Newport Beach, CA 92653
Ph. 949.261.7857
Fx. 949.261.5966
damion@damionhickman.com
www.damionhickman.com

	1
design firm	Damion Hickman Design
designer	Damion Hickman
client	Damion Hickman Design
software/hardware	Adobe Illustrator

	2
design firm	David Clark Design
designer	David Clark
client	Iron Werx
software/hardware	Adobe Illustrator

	3
design firm	Form Fuenf Bremen
art director	Daniel Henry Bastian
designer	Daniel Henry Bastian
client	Bautec GmbH
software/hardware	Adobe Illustrator, QuarkXPress
paper/materials	Gohrsmuehle Hadernhaltig 250 gsm
printing	Offset

1

2

iron werx

terry dixon   918.605.8993

1509 east 11th

tulsa, ok 74120

Creative graphic design solutions

Publishing
Corporate & Brand Communications
Logo & Identity
Signage & 3D

kf

1

kf design

群馬県高崎市高関町385 #401 〒370-0043
Takazeki-machi 385 #401
Takasaki, Gunma 370-0043

T 027 320 8300   F 027 320 8301
kevin@kfdesign.jp   www.kfdesign.jp

Kevin Foley
ケビン・フォリー

1

design firm	KF Design
art director	Kevin Foley
designer	Kevin Foley
client	KF Design
software/hardware	Adobe Illustrator, Mac
paper/materials	Arjo Wiggins Conqueror
printing	2 color

2

design firm	Wow! A Branding Company
art director	Dann Ilicic
designer	Will Johnson
client	Verb Exchange
software/hardware	Adobe Illustrator, Mac G4
printing	Classic Printing

nathanael lineham
president & ceo

[[[www.verbx.com]]]

tagline 877.574.4196
The best way to get me.

201-1166 Alberni Street Vancouver, BC V6E 3Z3
p. 604.685.8363   e. nat@verbx.com

[[[verb]]]
exchange

Your call to action.

VANCOUVER | PHOENIX

2

SILVERLIGHT RECORDS

MICHEL BITAR DeFAN
A&R MANAGER

1079 LEROY ST. SAN DIEGO CA 92106
619.795.0883 858.922.6367 619.795.0882

cheech@silverlightrecords.com
SILVERLIGHTRECORDS.COM

3

design firm	Justin Skeesuck Design Studio
art director	Justin Skeesuck
designer	Justin Skeesuck
client	Silverlight Records
software/hardware	Adobe Illustrator
paper/materials	French Smart White
printing	Hal Trushke Letterpress

4

design firm	Matter
art directors	Rick Griffith, Jason C. Otero
client	American Wilderness
software/hardware	Adobe Illustrator, Adobe Photoshop, QuarkXPress
printing	2-color offset

solutions for visual communications
23906 E. SECOND ST. ▶ GRAND RAPIDS.OH ▶ 43522
sisu4u@adelphia.net

419.832.6049

1

SiSU
design
(sis-su) tenacity of purpose

Jennifer Stucker
designer ▶ owner

	1
design firm	SiSU Design
art director	Jennifer Stucker
designer	Jennifer Stucker
illustrator	Jennifer Stucker
client	SiSU Design
software/hardware	Macromedia Freehand
paper/materials	Hammermill Via bright white
printing	1-color Pantone 2748, hand embossing

	2
design firm	Pure Imagination Studios
art director	Josh Williams
designer	Josh Williams
illustrator	Josh Williams
client	Customer Relations Company
software/hardware	Macromedia Freehand, Mac
paper/materials	Strathmore cover wove
printing	Lithographics Services, Inc.

Nathan O'Bryon
Owner

tel/fax: 630.850.7421
nobryon@aol.com

P.O. Box 127
Hinsdale, IL 60522

Customer Relations
C O M P A N Y

2

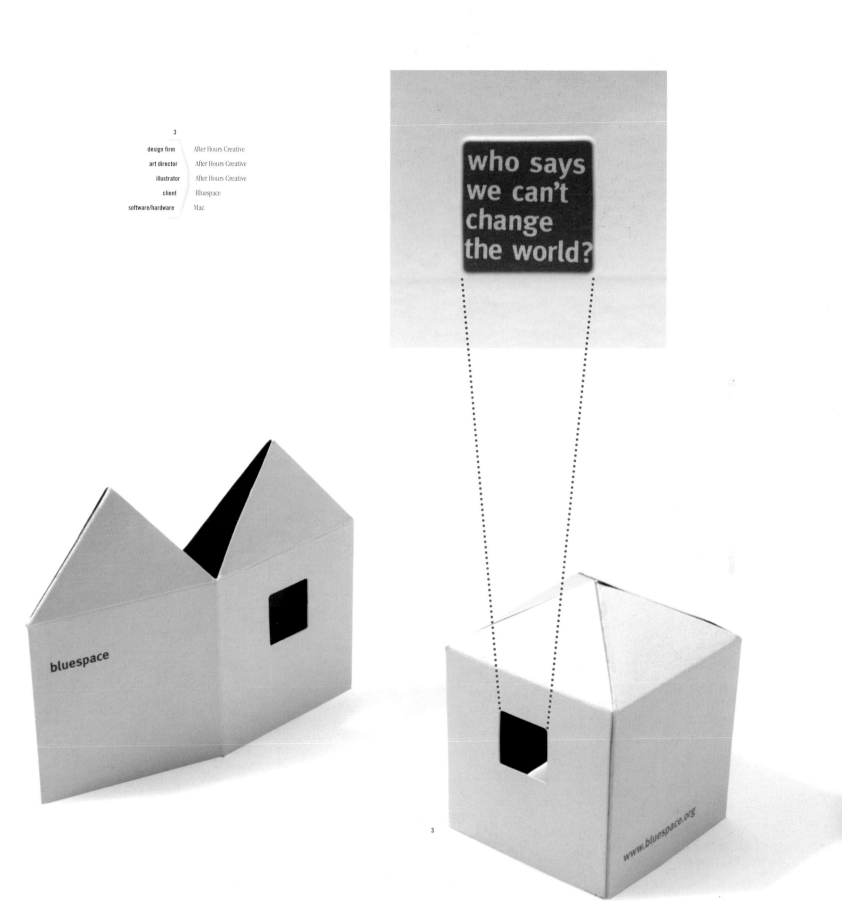

3	
design firm	After Hours Creative
art director	After Hours Creative
illustrator	After Hours Creative
client	Bluespace
software/hardware	Mac

who says
we can't
change
the world?

bluespace

www.bluespace.org

3

	1
design firm	Form Fuenf Bremen
art director	Daniel Henry Bastian
designer	Daniel Henry Bastian
client	Scharf. Rechts Anwälte
software/hardware	QuarkXPress
paper/materials	Plano Jet 300 gsm
printing	Offset

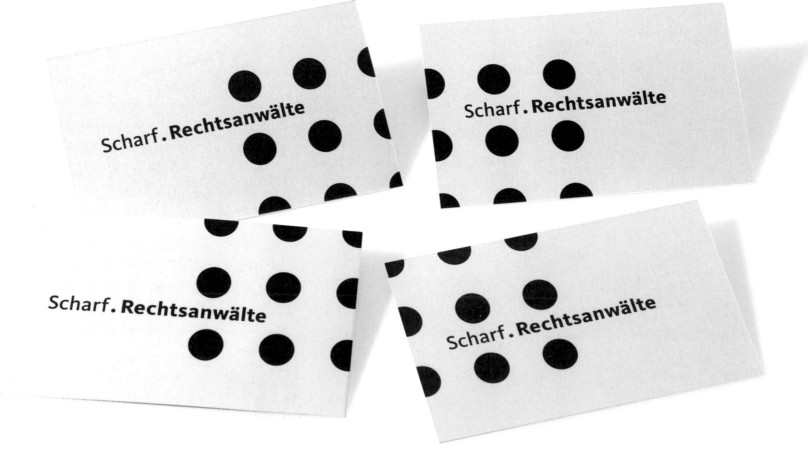

Hans-Wilhelm Koch
Rechtsanwalt
Fachanwalt für Familienrecht

Rechtsanwälte:
Dr. Ulrich Scharf
Dr. Wolfgang Burrack
Hans-Wilhelm Koch
D.-Joachim Klein
Friedrich-Wilhelm Hindahl
Christiane Greiner-Braschke
Stefan Obst
Kirsten Reimers
Timm Gottschalk

Weisser Wall 1
29221 Celle

Telefon 05141 9063-0
Telefax 05141 906326

kanzlei@scharfrechtsanwaelte.de
www.scharfrechtsanwaelte.de

1

MATTHEW L. BLEVINS

p 410 342 1214 x 223
e mlb@apexseo.com

results that drive success

APEX

913 S. Lakewood Ave.
Baltimore, MD 21224
p 410 342 1214
f 410 342 6341
1 800 324 1166

apex search engine marketing

info@apexseo.com
www.apexseo.com

2

design firm	re: salzman designs
art director	Ida Cheinman
designers	Ida Cheinman, Rick Salzman
client	Apex SEO
software/hardware	Adobe Illustrator, Mac
paper/materials	Mohawk Navajo double-thick 100 lb. cover
printing	2-color offset, 2 sided, die cut; London Litho

3

design firm	Rick Johnson & Company
designer	Tim McGrath
client	Crusty Underwear
software/hardware	Adobe Illustrator, QuarkXPress
paper/materials	Neenah Classic Crest
printing	Offset, color labels

GABRIEL SALAZAR

owner

5812 POJOAQUE RD. NE
ALBUQUERQUE, NEW MEXICO 87110

Ph 505.872.2045

Fx 505.872.9197

gabe@crustyunderwear.com

crusty underwear™

2

3

Ron Gillies

Lone Cypress Imp
4231 Witherby Stree
San Diego, California
+1 619 294 3978 ph
+1 619 990 4140 mob
ron.gillies@lonecypressin
www.lonecypressimporte

EST. 09·01

Lone Cypress

IMPORTERS

PURVEYORS OF FINE WINES

SAN DIEGO, CA

WINE ME

eep, intense purple/red, ...que almost to rim. A spur...
...ng wine, from the first impact of the nose...m th...
...ng, long finish. Sweet, intense and...flavours...
...ackcurrants, plums and mulberries layered with toba...

GRETCHEN ROSS

[7 MORNINGSIDE AVE, UPPER MONTCLAIR, NJ 07043]

TEL 917.750.5216

[CARSON VASQUEZ PHOTOGRAPHY]

	1
design firm	Miriello Grafico, Inc.
art director	Ron Miriello
designer	Dennis Garcia
illustrator	Dennis Garcia
client	Lone Cypress Importers
software/hardware	Adobe Illustrator
paper/materials	Neenah Classic Crest
printing	Rush Press

	2
design firm	Tom & John: A Design Collaborative
art directors	Tom Sizu, John Givens
designers	Tom Sizu, John Givens
illustrator	Tom Sizu
client	Carson Vasquez Photography
software/hardware	Adobe Illustrator, Mac
printing	Offset

alittlebiz

	3	
design firm		Gardner Design
art director		Bill Gardner
client		alittlebiz
software/hardware		Macromedia Freehand
printing		Printmaster, 2 color, angled trim

	4	
design firm		Wow! A Branding Company
art director		Perry Chua
designer		Will Johnson
client		NGRAIN
software/hardware		Adobe Illustrator, Mac G4
printing		Generation Printing

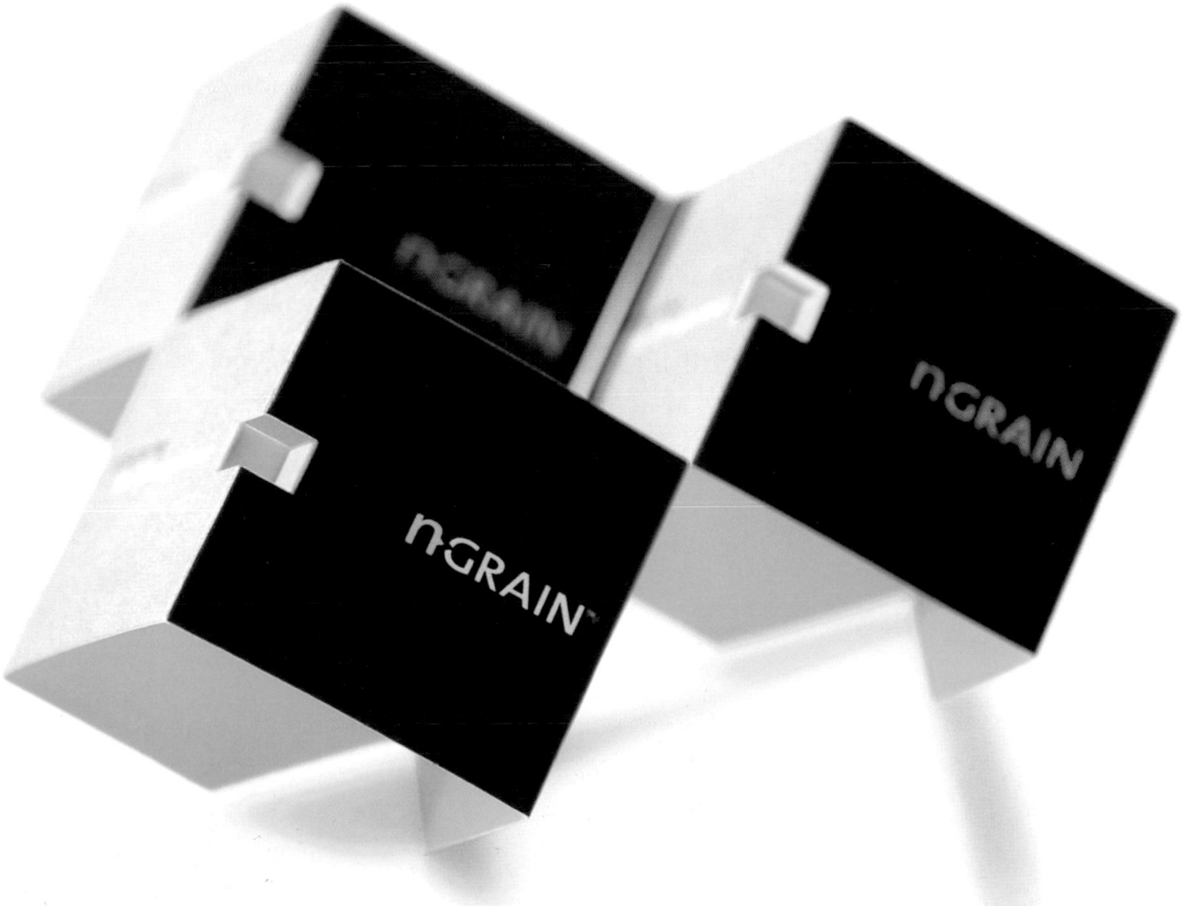

Intuitive
adjective: innate, instinctive, natural

Jordana Nepon
Account Coordinator
jordana@aerialpr.com

Aerial Communications Group Inc
970A Eglinton Avenue West
Toronto, Ontario M6C 2C5
T 416.787.6577 ext.32
F 416.787.6544

www.aerialpr.com

Original
noun: imaginative, creative, fresh, clever, unique

Anne Yourt
Account Executive
anne@aerialpr.com

Aerial Communications Group Inc.
970A Eglinton Avenue West
Toronto, Ontario M6C 2C5
T 416.787.6577 ext.22
F 416.787.654

Integrity
noun: honesty, moral, principle, straightforwardness

Roanne Goldsman
Financial Director
roanne@aerialpr.com

Aerial Communications Group Inc.
970A Eglinton Avenue West
Toronto, Ontario M6C 2C5
T 416.787.6577 ext.22
F 416.787.6544

www.aerialpr.com

Lauren Dineen
Account Coordinator
lauren@aerialpr.com

AERIAL
COMMUNICATIONS GROUP

...ications Group Inc.
...West

Dynamic
adjective: active, vital, energetic, driving, powerful

Influential
adjective: effective, instrumental, forceful, inspiring

Naomi Strasser
President
naomi@aerialpr.com

AERIAL
COMMUNICATIONS GROUP

Aerial Communications Group Inc.
970A Eglinton Avenue West
Toronto, Ontario M6C 2C5
T 416.787.6577 ext.21
F 416.787.6544

www.aerialpr.com

Jefferson Darrell
Account Manager
jefferson@aerialpr.com

AERIAL
COMMUNICATIONS GROUP

Aerial Communications Group Inc.
970A Eglinton Avenue West
Toronto, Ontario M...
T 416 78...

Rapport
noun: relationship, understanding, affiliation, connection

design firm	ARTiculation Group
art director	Joseph Chan
designer	Joseph Chan
illustrator	Joseph Chan
client	Aerial Communications Group Inc.
software/hardware	Adobe Illustrator, Mac G3, G4
paper/materials	McCoy Silk
printing	Offset

pink+purple public relations

Claudia Lüders

Leinpfad 80   22299 Hamburg
Tel.:+49(0)40-460 90 501   Fax:+49(0)40-460 90 502
c.lueders@pink-purple.de

1

JUDY MATTERA
pastry chef

the federalist
FIFTEEN BEACON
15 beacon street
boston massachusetts 02108-2902
telephone 617.670.2515
fax 617.670.2526

2

1

design firm	Marius Fahrner Design
art director	Marius Fahrner
designer	Marius Fahrner
illustrator	Marius Fahrner
client	Pink + Purple Public Relations
software/hardware	Macromedia Freehand
printing	2-color Pantone offset

2

design firm	plus design, inc.
art director	Anita Meyer
designer	Anita Meyer
client	The Federalist
paper/materials	Crane's Crest florescent white 110 lb. cover
printing	Artcraft

RE|invent

fx 919.835.1510 | www.jdavisarchitects.com | 510 Glenwood Ave. Ste. 201 Raleigh, NC 27603

3

3	
design firm	Forma Design
art director	David Chapin
designer	Nancy Schruers
client	J. Davis Arcitects
software/hardware	Macromedia Freehand, Mac
paper/materials	Gilbert Esse Smooth, 80 lb.
printing	Carter Printing, offset

4	
design firm	Mirage Design
art director	Mark DaPonte
designer	Lynette Allaire
client	Natural Nails Spa
software/hardware	Macromedia Freehand

JDAVISARCHITECTS

Jeffrey T. Davis, AIA
President

jeff@jdavisarchitects.com | 919.835.1500

Natural Nails Spa
Appointment
For
Day   Date   Time
31 Louise F. Luther Drive, Cumberland, RI 02864 phone 401.334.0453

Natural Nails Spa   Michelle Ward
31 Louise F. Luther Drive, Cumberland, Rhode Island 02864
phone 401.334.0453, email mcward3@home.com

4

Natural Nails Spa

1

design firm	M-Art
art director	Marty Ittner
designer	Marty Ittner
client	M-Art
software/hardware	Adobe Photoshop, QuarkXPress
paper/materials	Monadnock Astrolite
printing	Dickson's

2

design firm	Momentum Press and Design
art director	Jill Vartenigian
designer	Jill Vartenigian
client	Rejuvenate Massage
paper/materials	Speckletone; handset lead type and dingbat
printing	Letterpress; Chandler and Price Letterpress

brainstorm

M-Art | Marty Ittner
301·588·8591

marty@m-art.org   FAX 301·588·8592
7902 FLOWER AVENUE · TAKOMA PARK, MD 20912

REJUVENATION
ON-SITE MASSAGE & SOUND THERAPY
Special Events & Work Place

Kathleen Rall-Tseng, Owner
206.226.0106   1714 N 45th Str

REJUVENATION
MASSAGE & SOUND THERAPY
at Salon Metro

Kathleen Rall-Tseng, LMP
206.226.0106   1714 N 45th Street • Seattle, WA 98103

soulful | strong | sensual

MAVEN

MAVEN

SANDI HWANG
Chief Executive Officer

T 312.782.6240   F 312.551.0506
36 S Wabash Ste 1415 Chicago, IL 60603 USA
sandi@mavencosmetics.com
www.mavencosmetics.com

3

design firm	Brainforest, Inc.
art director	Nils Bunde
designer	David Pfluger
client	Maven Cosmetics
software/hardware	QuarkXPress
paper/materials	Mohawk Superfine
printing	client

4

design firm	Wilson Harvey
art director	Paul Burgess
designer	Paul Burgess
client	Ratio One
software/hardware	Adobe Illustrator, QuarkXPress, Mac
paper/materials	Art board 350 gsm
printing	2-color lithography

TOM.CARTWRIGHT@RATIOONE.COM
WWW.RATIOONE.COM

SIR JOHN LYON HOUSE
5 HIGH TIMBER STREET
BLACKFRIARS
LONDON
EC4V 3NX

DDI   020 7557 4762
TEL   020 7557 4760
FAX   020 7557 4768
MOB 0770 315 8088

PAUL GRAVILLE
TECHNICAL DIRECTOR

ACCESSORIES

CHRISTOPH
Agent Men

RENÉ LEZARD

REINHOLD SCHEIDT
Geschäftsführer

Kaiser
Fax +
ww

RENÉ LEZARD Mode GmbH
Industriestraße 2 D-97359 Schwarzach Telefon +49/9324-302-112
Fax +49/9324-302-114 www.rene-lezard.com R.scheidt@rene-lezard.de

1

1

design firm	Simon & Goetz Design
art director	Pia Kemper
designer	Pia Kemper
client	René Lezard
software/hardware	Macromedia Freehand, Mac
paper/materials	Distinction Edition Strahlendweiß
printing	Offset

2

design firm	Goodesign
designers	Kathryn Hammill, Diane Shaw
client	Goodesign
software/hardware	QuarkXPress
paper/materials	Starwhite Tiara double-thick cover

FIND   DIANE SHAW   SEND   4 W. 37TH ST, NYC 10018
CALL   646 473 1520   VISIT   GOODESIGNNY.COM
FAX   646 473 1519   WRITE   DIANE@GOODESIGNNY.COM

goodesign

2

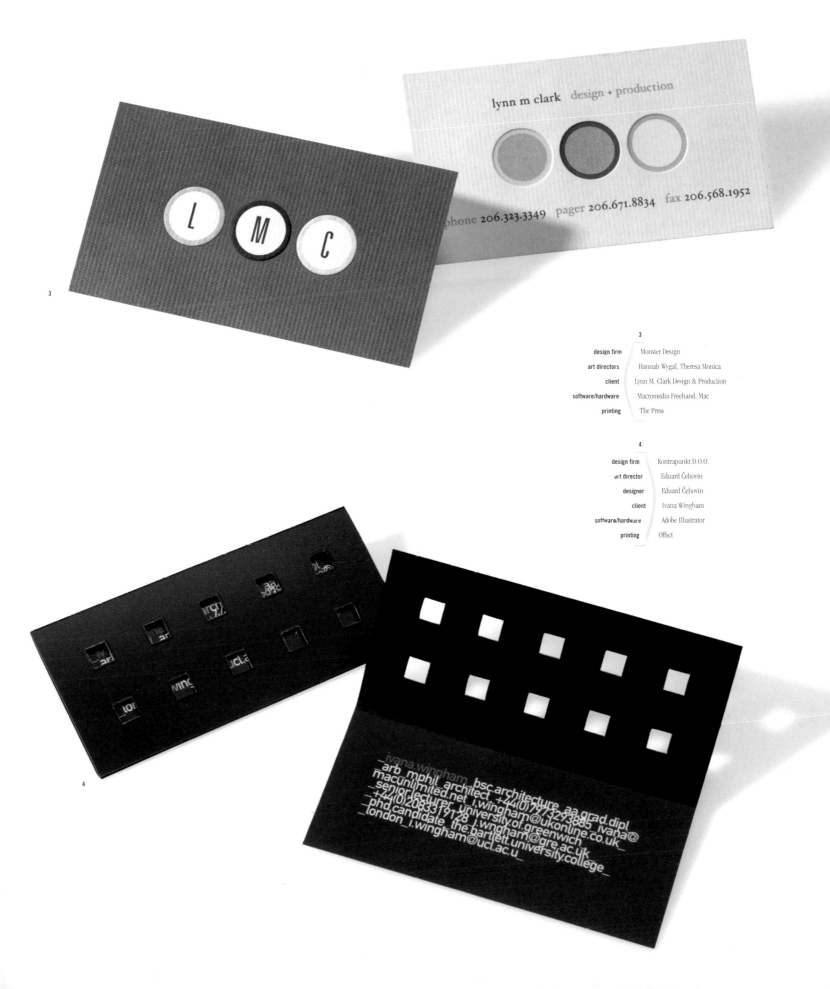

3

design firm	Monster Design
art directors	Hannah Wygal, Theresa Monica
client	Lynn M. Clark Design & Production
software/hardware	Macromedia Freehand, Mac
printing	The Press

4

design firm	Kontrapunkt D.O.O.
art director	Eduard Čehovin
designer	Eduard Čehovin
client	Ivana Wingham
software/hardware	Adobe Illustrator
printing	Offset

lynn m clark design + production

phone 206.323.3349   pager 206.671.8834   fax 206.568.1952

_ivana.wingham _bsc.architecture _aa.grad.dipl
_arb _mphil _architect _i.wingham +44(0)7973293885 _ivana@
macunlimited.net _i.wingham@ukonline.co.uk_
_senior.lecturer _university.of.greenwich
+44(0)20831 9128 _i.wingham@gre.ac.uk_
_phd.candidate _the.bartlett.university.college_
london_ i.wingham@ucl.ac.u_

LE CAFÉ SOLEIL

Le Café Soleil is a quick service café style restaurant in Georgetown that focuses on healthy, high-energy food.

MENU SELECTIONS:

FRESH FRUIT SMOOTHIES

ROCKET JUICE

SPECIALTY HOT BEVERAGES

WRAPS

SALADS

GRILLED SANDWICHES

MENU OF SERVICES:
NUTRITIONAL CONSULTATION
COOKING CLASSES
LIFESTYLE CHANGE WORKSHOPS

(905) 877-2677

LE CAFÉ SOLEIL

nancy desjardins

78 MAIN ST. SOUTH
GEORGETOWN
ONTARIO L7G 3G3
(905) 877-2677
soleil@downtowngeorgetown.com

www.freshproductdesign.com

FRESH

FRESH ™
PRODUCT DESIGN

derek pyner
Vice President Electrical Design
pyner@freshproductdesign.com

8505 Eastlake Drive Burnaby BC, Canada V5A 4T7
p 800.561.3322 **p** 604.421.1311 ext 20 **f** 604.421.9202
IN PARTNERSHIP WITH PDE

1	
design firm	Mindwalk Design Group, Inc.
art director	Michael Huggins, RGD
designer	Nicole Pineau
client	Le Café Soleil
software/hardware	Adobe Illustrator, Macromedia Freehand, QuarkXPress
paper/materials	Classic Laid Ivorystone 80 lb. cover
printing	Print This

2	
design firm	Wow! A Branding Company
art director	Will Johnson
designer	Will Johnson
client	Fresh Product Design
software/hardware	Adobe Illustrator, Mac G4
printing	Classic Printing

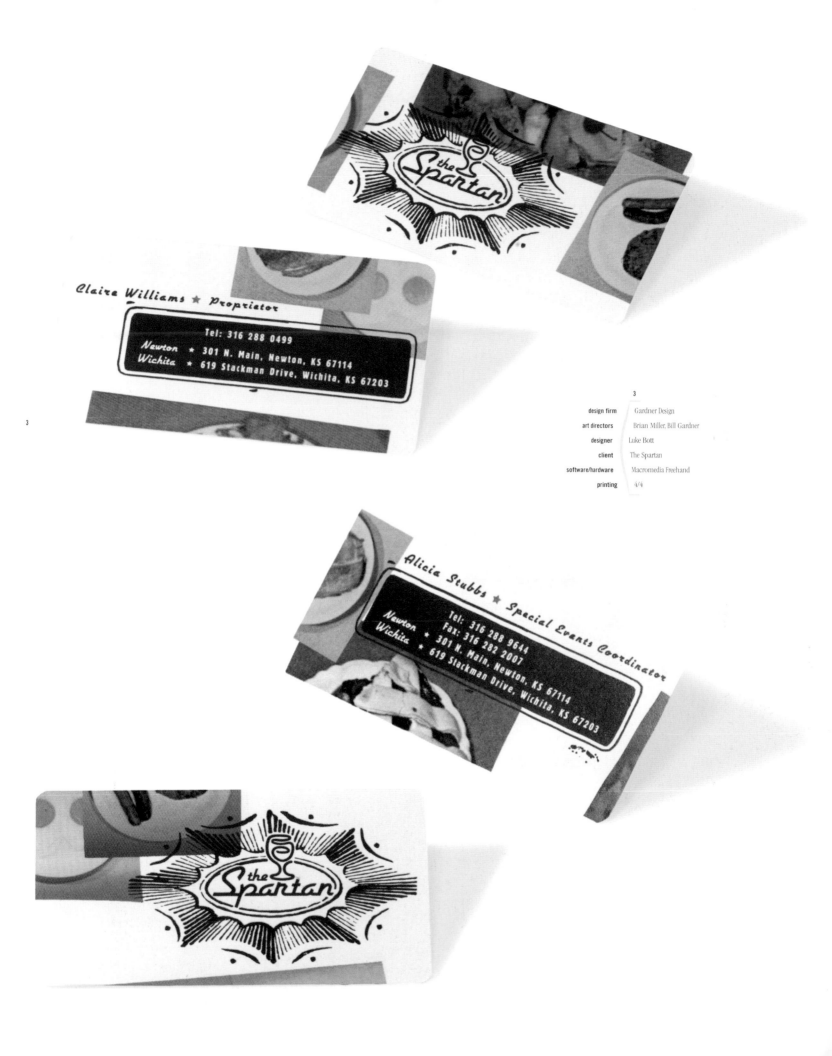

Claire Williams ★ Proprietor

Tel: 316 288 0499
Newton ★ 301 N. Main, Newton, KS 67114
Wichita ★ 619 Stackman Drive, Wichita, KS 67203

the Spartan

Alicia Stubbs ★ Special Events Coordinator

Tel: 316 288 9644
Fax: 316 282 2007
Newton ★ 301 N. Main, Newton, KS 67114
Wichita ★ 619 Stackman Drive, Wichita, KS 67203

the Spartan

3

design firm	Gardner Design
art directors	Brian Miller, Bill Gardner
designer	Luke Bott
client	The Spartan
software/hardware	Macromedia Freehand
printing	4/4

3

	1
design firm	Riordon Design
art director	Dan Wheaton
designer	Alan Krpan
client	Interpix Design Inc.
software/hardware	Adobe Illustrator, QuarkXPress
paper/materials	Neenah Classic Crest solar white 110 lb. cover
printing	CJ Graphics

1

Cathy Kealey · Information Architect
cathy@interpixdesign.com

Interpix Design Inc.
1101 Clarkson Road North, Suite 302
Mississauga, Ontario L5J 2W1
T 905.403.0401 C 416.577.3462

www.interpixdesign.com

	2
design firm	Glitschka Studios
art director	Von R. Glitschka
designer	Von R. Glitschka
illustrator	Von R. Glitschka
client	Joe Mocha
software/hardware	Macromedia Freehand, Mac G4
paper/materials	Environment Cover Tortilla
printing	2 spot colors

2

Leanne Bennett-Jones
Food Consultant & Stylist
Special Events & Promotions Coordinator

Demonstration Kitchen Hire

29 Hawkes Road
North Warrandyte
Victoria 3113 Australia
Telephone: 613) 9844 1849
Facsimile: 613) 9844 3271
Mobile: 0417 559 447
Email: cuisine@plumbpie.com
www.plumbpie.com

3

Cuisine Collection

Leanne Bennett-Jones

design firm	Octavo Design
art director	Gary Domoney
client	Cuisine Collection
software/hardware	Adobe Illustrator, Mac
paper/materials	White A artboard 360 gsm
printing	2 color, black and bronze, plus embossing

4

design firm	CPd
art director	Chris Perks
designer	Mauric Lai
client	Hyphen Consulting
software/hardware	Adobe Illustrator
paper/materials	Spicers Starwhite Smooth 297 gsm
printing	3-color PMS, gloss varnish

Steven Raynes-Greenow
Director

Hyphen   Hyphen Consulting

13 Warley Road Malvern East Victoria 3145
T 03 9572 3126 F 03 9572 3548 M 0413 870 766
E sraynesgreenow@bigpond.com.au

4

SKIN
BIOLOGY
CENTER

B·C

MED. VOLKER STEI

design firm	Marius Fahrner Design
art director	Marius Fahrner
designer	Marius Fahrner
illustrator	Marius Fahrner
client	Skin Biology Center
software/hardware	Macromedia Freehand
paper/materials	Roeemerturm Precioso 250 gsm
printing	2-color Pantone offset

S·B·C

SKIN
BIOLOGY
CENTER

PROF. DR. MED. VOLKER STEINKRAUS

Dammtorwall 4 | 20354 Hamburg

Telefon 040.350 90 33 | Telefax 040.350 90 350

1

design firm	iamalwayshungry
art director	Nessim Higson
designer	Nessim Higson
illustrator	Nessim Higson
client	iamalwayshungry
software/hardware	Adobe Illustrator
paper/materials	Strathmore Avalanche
printing	Offset

1

katala@dm.net.lb

2

Joumana Ghandour Atallah   Architecture & Urban Design
Avenue des Français . PO Box 1084 . Beirut Lebanon . P 03 377 878 . F 01 373 370

	2
design firm	Nassar Design
art director	Nélida Nassar
designer	Nélida Nassar
client	Joumana Ghandour Atallah Architecture & Urban Design
software/hardware	QuarkXPress
paper/materials	Ivoline High Speed white 300 gsm
printing	Alpha Press

	3
design firm	Kolegram Design
art director	Mike Teixeira
designer	Mike Teixeira
client	Axeneór Artist's Centre
software/hardware	Adobe Illustrator, QuarkXPress
paper/materials	Fraser Pegasus
printing	Du Progrès

CENTRE D'ARTISTES

80, RUE FRONT, HULL/GATINEAU (QUÉBEC) J8Y 3M5
819.771.2122 TÉLÉCOPIEUR 819.771.0696
AXENEO7@AXENEO7.QC.CA WWW.AXENEO7.QC.CA

3

corporate literature
corporate identity
advertising & promotions

design

zucchini design pte ltd 30a mosque street singapore 059508
tel.6887 5746 fax.6223 8070 hp.9852 8428 email.betty@zucchini.com.sg

betty soh
account director

zucchini

1

design firm	Zucchini Design Pte. Ltd.
art director	Tew Sun Ne
designer	Tew Sun Ne
client	Zucchini Design Pte. Ltd.
software/hardware	Macromedia Freehand
paper/materials	Keaykolour galvanized 250 gsm
printing	Octogram Pte. Ltd.

2

design firm	Gardner Design
designer	Brian Miller
client	Modern Salon Services
software/hardware	Macromedia Freehand
printing	Printmaster, 2 metallic colors

modern_salon_services

pilar_cortes

1212_VALLEY_RIDGE_DRIVE
GRAIN_VALLEY_MO_64029_
214_535_4166_MOBILE_TEL
888_658_1761_CORPORATE
816_847_0323_FACSIMILE_

BLUE PRAIRIE
— Group —

INSTITUTIONAL
RETIREMENT CONSULTING
AND RESEARCH

www.blueprairiegroup.com

3

design firm	Brainforest, Inc.
art director	Nils Bunde
designer	Drew Larson
client	Blue Prairie Group
software/hardware	Adobe Illustrator, QuarkXPress
paper/materials	Mohawk Superfine
printing	Active Graphics

4

design firm	Grapefruit Design
art director	Marius Ursache
designer	Marius Ursache
client	Grapefruit Design
software/hardware	Adobe Illustrator, Adobe Photoshop, Photodisc
paper/materials	Garda Matte 350 gsm
printing	Poligrafia Codex

Matthew Gnabasik
PRESIDENT
matt@ blueprairiegroup.com

IRIE

BLUE PRAIRIE GROUP, L.L.C.
440 NORTH WELLS, SUITE 550
CHICAGO, IL 60610
www.blueprairiegroup.com

BLU

GENERAL: (312)645-1899
DIRECT: (312)645-1120
TOLL FREE: (866)274-1899
FAX: (312)467-1899

Marius Ursache
Chief Creative Officer

Str. Gării 5, BL.L17, Ap.1, Iași IS 6600, Romania
T/F: 032.233068 (RO)   M: 094.863740 (MOBILE)
T/F: 646.349.2916 (US)   T/F: 0870.127.5996 (UK)
ICQ: 44647986   E: marius@grapefruitdesign.com
WEB: www.grapefruitdesign.com

GRAPEFRUIT
DESIGN

design firm	Wallace Church, Inc.
art director	Stan Church
designer	Nin Glaister
client	Wallace Church, Inc.
software/hardware	Adobe Illustrator, Adobe Photoshop
paper/materials	Mohawk
printing	Karr Graphics

WALLACE CHURCH

WALLACE CHURCH

WALLACE CHURCH.

WALLACE CHURCH

Wallace Church, Inc.
Strategic Brand Identity
330 East 48th Street
New York, NY 10017
1 212 755 2903
F 212 355 6872
stan@wallacechurch.com

STANLEY CHURCH
Managing Partner
Creative

riordondesign   (inform)inspire(

Ric Riordon
corporate director

905.339.0750 x22
ric@riordondesign.com

131 George Street
Oakville, ON L6J 3B9

1	
design firm	Riordon Design
art director	Dan Wheaton
designers	Dan Wheaton, Alan Krpan
client	Riordon Design
software/hardware	Adobe Illustrator, QuarkXPress
paper/materials	Benefit Blue Yonder 80 lb. cover,
	duplexed to Raisin Cane 80 lb. cover
printing	Anstey Book Binding (letterpress)

2	
design firm	Bandujo Donker & Brothers
art director	Robert Brothers Jr.
illustrator	Bandujo Donker & Brothers
software/hardware	Adobe Illustrator, QuarkXPress
paper/materials	McCoy Matte 120 lb.

BANDUJO DONKER & BROTHERS
advertising and design

BANDUJO DONKER & BROTHERS | advertising and design

todd goodman 396 springfield ave summit nj 07901
t.908.608.2032 c.973.960.7893 f.908.608.2030
tgoodman@bandujo.com   www.bandujo.com

1

2

Buzz
Strategic Insights Pty Ltd

3/7 O'Brien Street
Bondi
New South Wales 2026
Australia

Telephone 61 2 9369 4400
Facsimile 61 2 9369 4305
theteam@buzzsi.com.au
www.buzzsi.com.au

Nina Finlayson
Director

Mobile 0413 306 360
nina@buzzsi.com.au

buzz
strategic insights

3

	3
design firm	CPd
art director	Nigel Beechey (Sydney)
designer	Nigel Beechey
finished artwork	Aggie Rozycka
client	Buzz Strategic Insights
software/hardware	Adobe Illustrator
paper/materials	Rapier Deluxe 310 gsm
printing	2 special PMS, matte lamination

	4
design firm	Debenham Design Inc.
art director	Eileen Debenham
designer	Yuko Inagaki
client	Debenham Design Inc.
software/hardware	Adobe Illustrator
paper/materials	Benefit 80 lb. vertical cover
printing	Reynolds-Dewalt Printing

D
inc
debenham design inc.

gareth debenham | principal

debenham design inc.
3rd floor 200 highland avenue
needham ma 02494 usa
(t) 781 444 8515 x23   (f) 781 444 8560
(e) gareth@debenhamdesign.com

D
inc

4

design inspired ideas

design inspired ideas

design5

ron nikkel

7636 n ingram 102
fresno ca 93711
559 432 5110
559 432 6158 fax
ron@designfive.com
designfive.com

1

design firm	Design 5
art director	Ron Nikkel
designer	Ron Nikkel
client	Design 5
software/hardware	Adobe Illustrator, Mac G4
printing	Offset

2

design firm	Get Smart Design Co.
art director	GSDC Staff, Robin MacFarlane
designers	Jeff MacFarlane
client	That's My Dog!
software/hardware	Adobe Photoshop, Macromedia Freehand, QuarkXPress, Mac
paper/materials	Strobe
printing	Tristate Graphics

www.thatsmydog.biz

That's My Dog!
★ Problem Solving
★ Obedience
★ Behavior Modification
★ Personal Protection
★ Puppy Preschool
★ Board & Train Services

★ Boarding Available

ROBIN MACFARLANE
Training Director
robin@thatsmydog.biz

That's My Dog!
SUPER TRAINING FOR
EVERYDAY ADVENTURES

1619 Highway 11
Hazel Green, WI 53811
608.854.2062

www.thatsmydog.biz

3

design firm	M-Art
art director	Marty Ittner
designer	Marty Ittner
client	Big Cheese Light
software/hardware	QuarkXPress
paper/materials	Gmund Bier Ale
printing	Printing Services, Inc.

3

4

design firm	Collaborated, Inc.
art directors	James Evelock, Tony Leone
designer	James Evelock
client	Collaborated, Inc.
software/hardware	Adobe Illustrator
paper/materials	Expressions uncoated cover 130 lb.
printing	Pride Printers

4

design firm	Lewis Communications/Nashville
art director	Robert Froedge
designer	Robert Froedge
illustrator	Robert Froedge
client	Ivy Park
software/hardware	Adobe Illustrator, QuarkXPress
paper/materials	French Speckletone
printing	1-color plus letterpress

Angela Irvine, Ph.D.
principal

phone 831 345 5336
email angelairvine@cerespolicyresearch.com
web www.cerespolicyresearch.com

1

cerespolicyresearch

ansata
therapeutics

2

T. Richard Lin, Ph.D.
Research Investigator

505 Coast Blvd. South
La Jolla, CA 92037
P 858.754.3017
F 858.754.3001
richard@ansatainc.com

Accentuate Inc.
15320 Cornet Avenue
Santa Fe Springs, CA 90670

ph 562.404.4976
ph 714.532.3015
fx 562.921.7038

www.accentuateinc.com
lschiada@accentuateinc.com

Laurie Schiada
VP Creative

3

accentuate
INC

3	
design firm	Accentuate Inc.
art director	Laurie Schiada
designers	Danny Tongsand, Bret Chambers
client	Accentuate Inc.
software/hardware	Adobe Illustrator
paper/materials	Endeavour velvet cover 130 lb.

4	
design firm	Gateway Arts
art director	Dave Carlson
designer	Dave Carlson
client	Gateway Arts
software/hardware	Adobe Illustrator
paper/materials	100 lb. cover
printing	3/2

GATEWAY ARTS

810 LAWRENCE DRIVE #220
THOUSAND OAKS, CA 91320
WWW.GATEWAYARTS.COM

PHONE (805) 480-1140 x207
FAX (805) 480-1150
DAVE@GATEWAYARTS.COM

DAVE CARLSON • CREATIVE DIRECTOR

THE CHALLENGE TO CREATE AND INSPIRE.

4

CHEVEUX

3700 N. WOODLAWN
SUITE NUMBER 103
WICHITA, KAN 67220

HAIRCUTS
COLOR
TEXTURE
DRESSWORK

THIS TIME

day

time

service

products

mindy TABLER

HAIR
STYLIST

p»(316)312-6588

mop
modern organic products

alfaPARF
milano

1

Jalan Merpati Raya 45, Jakarta 12870, Indonesia

Lans Brahmantyo
Creative Director

phone 62.21.8306819 fax 62.21.8290612 mobile
e-mail brahm@afterhoursgroup.com

afterhours
JAKARTA

www.afterhoursgroup.com

2

1

design firm	Gardner Design
designer	Brian Miller
client	Amber Lear Salon
software/hardware	Macromedia Freehand
printing	Printmaster, 3 color

2

design firm	Afterhours Group
art director	Lans Brahmantyo
designer	Fedra Carina Meredith
client	Afterhours Group
software/hardware	Adobe InDesign, Adobe Illustrator
paper/materials	Fox River, Arjo Wiggins
printing	Coronado, Iridescent, Standar Grafika

design firm	Wilson Harvey
art director	Paul Burgess
designer	Ben Wood
illustrator	Ben Wood
client	Bang Creations
software/hardware	Adobe Illustrator, QuarkXPress, Mac
paper/materials	Art board 350 gsm
printing	4-color lithography

Tobias Schaible
Veranstaltungen
Fortbildungen

Schloss Kapfenburg
D 73466 Lauchheim

Fon +49 73 63 96 18 17
Fax +49 73 63 96 18 20

Sabine Maier
Notenhaus

Schloss Kapfenburg
D 73466 Lauchheim

Fon +49 73 63 91 98 80
Fax +49 73 63 91 98 81

Hermann Holzmeier
Hausverwalter

Schloss Kapfenburg
D 73466 Lauchheim

Fon +49 73 63 96 18 14
Fax +49 73 63 96 18 20

Katharina Mallach
Probenaufenthalte
Buchungen

Schloss Kapfenburg
D 73466 Lauchheim

Fon +49 73 63 96 18 14
Fax +49 73 63 96 18 20

Nicole Stark
Öffentlichkeitsarbeit
Internationale Projekte

Schloss Kapfenburg
D 73466 Lauchheim

Fon +49 73 63 96 18 13
Fax +49 73 63 96 18 20

Ulrike Münter
Fortbildungen Veranstaltungen
Öffentlichkeitsarbeit

Schloss Kapfenburg
D 73466 Lauchheim

Fon +49 73 63 96 18 13
Fax +49 73 63 96 18 20

Bruno Weissenburger
Schlossverwalter

Schloss Kapfenburg
D 73466 Lauchheim

Fon +49 73 63 96 18 0
Fon +49 17 27 32 08
Fax +49 73 63 96 18 20

Michael Gunkel
Küchenmeister

Schloss Kapfenburg
D 73466 Lauchheim

Fon +49 73 63 96 99 40
Fax +49 73 63 96 99 49

Internationale
Musikschulakademie
Kulturzentrum
Schloss Kapfenburg

SchlossKapfenburg

www.schloss-kapfenburg.de
stollweber@schloss-kapfenburg.de

design firm	Baumann & Baumann
art directors	Barbara and Gerd Baumann
designers	Barbara and Gerd Baumann
illustrators	Barbara and Gerd Baumann
client	Schloss Kapfenburg
software/hardware	Macromedia Freehand
paper/materials	Conqueror
printing	Offset

design firm	Duffy Singapore
art director	Christopher Lee
designer	Christopher Lee
client	Yang Tan
software/hardware	Macromedia Freehand
paper/materials	2 mm technical board
printing	Deboss, foil stamping on all edges

YANGTAN
50 Battery Place #3Z New York NY 10280 USA
Phone 212.608.7451 Fax 212.608.5391
yang@yangtan.com

YANGTAN
50 Battery Place #3
Phone 212.608.151 Fax
yang@yangtan.com

429 PARTNERS

... DAVID GLASS PRINCIPAL

EMAIL DGLASS@429PARTNERS.COM

TEL 425 241 1355 FAX 530 236 7862 WEB 429PARTNERS.COM
1075 BELLEVUE WAY NE, SUITE 305 BELLEVUE, WA 98004

1

1

design firm	Function
designer	Jeff Culver
client	429 Partners
software/hardware	QuarkXPress
paper/materials	Crane's
printing	Letterpress

2

design firm	Chen Design Associates
art director	Joshua C. Chen
designer	Max Spector
illustrator	Max Spector
client	Collaborativisions
software/hardware	Adobe Illustrator, Mac
paper/materials	Mohawk Options True White 130 lb.
printing	Oscar Printing Co., 2 PMS, 2 sided

(415)564-0817
1241 Stanyan Street
San Francisco, California
94117-3816

elana@collaborativisions.com

collaborativisions
mediation and training services

Elana Auerbach Weiss

2

the studio of bryan boettiger
1339 27th Street, Denver CO 80202
303-332-6201

3

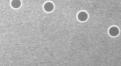

3

design firm	Matter
art director	Rick Griffith
illustrator	Rick Griffith
client	Bryan Boettiger
software/hardware	Adobe Illustrator, Adobe Photoshop, QuarkXPress
printing	4-color offset

4

design firm	re: salzman designs
art director	Ida Cheinman
designers	Ida Cheinman, Rick Salzman
client	Litecast
software/hardware	Adobe Illustrator, Mac
paper/materials	Strathmore Elements 100 lb. cover
printing	3-color offset, 2 sided, die cut, Hunt Valley Printing

LITECAST
Connect to Your Future

www.litecast.net
info@litecast.net

915 S. Lakewood Avenue
Baltimore, Maryland 21224

p 410 732 2756
f 443 267 0076

Mark Wagner
Chief Executive Officer

mark@litecast.net

4

1

design firm	Entermotion Design Studio
art director	Brian Cartwright
designer	Brian Cartwright
client	Wild Things Taxidermy
software/hardware	Macromedia Freehand, Mac
paper/materials	Kraff
printing	2-color screenprinting, enamel ink

2

design firm	Dan Elliott
designer	Dan Elliott
illustrator	Dan Elliott
client	Bite Sandwiches
software/hardware	Adobe Illustrator, QuarkXPress, Mac
paper/materials	Matte art board 350 gsm
printing	4 color

3

design firm	Firebelly Design Co.
art director	Dawn Hancock
designer	Dawn Hancock
client	Amy Walsh
software/hardware	Adobe Illustrator, Mac G4
printing	1-color letterpress, Rohner Letterpress

4

design firm	Blank, Inc.
art director	Robert Kent Wilson
designers	Robert Kent Wilson, Christine Dzieciolowski
client	Blank, Inc.
software/hardware	Adobe Illustrator, Mac G4
paper/materials	Finch Fine
printing	Fox Printing, Artisan (embossing)

jamie cooper
jamie@ajm.uk.net

JC

T. +44 (0)20 8941 0888 | F. +44 (0)20 8879 4805 | m. +44 (0)7768 461479
millennium house | 7 high street | hampton | middlesex | tw12 2sa | uk

1

1

design firm	Dan Elliott
designer	Dan Elliott
illustrator	Dan Elliott
client	Jamie Cooper
software/hardware	Adobe Illustrator, QuarkXPress, Mac
paper/materials	Matte art board 350 gsm
printing	1 color

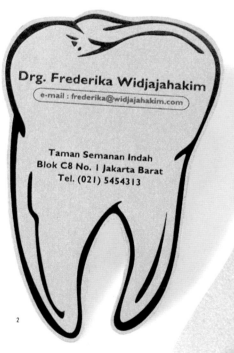

Drg. Frederika Widjajahakim
e-mail : frederika@widjajahakim.com

**Taman Semanan Indah
Blok C8 No. 1 Jakarta Barat
Tel. (021) 5454313**

2

2

design firm	Sapulidi Advertising & Gift Promotion
art director	Rudolf Widjajahakim
designer	Denny Hendriyanto
client	Dr. Frederika Widjajahakim
software/hardware	Macromedia Freehand, Mac G4
paper/materials	Curious Metallic Iridescent, virtual pearl, 240 gsm
printing	One-side screen printing

3

design firm	Emma Wilson Design Company
art director	Emma Wilson
client	Frontier Room Restaurant
software/hardware	Macromedia Freehand, Mac G4
paper/materials	Gilbert Voice white 100 lb. cover
printing	4/2, PMS 1525, PMS 109, black, dull varnish over black with dull varnish

4

design firm	Duck Soup Graphics, Inc.
art director	Bill Doucette
designer	Bill Doucette
client	Metrocore
software/hardware	Adobe Illustrator
paper/materials	Strathmore Elements
printing	3 color

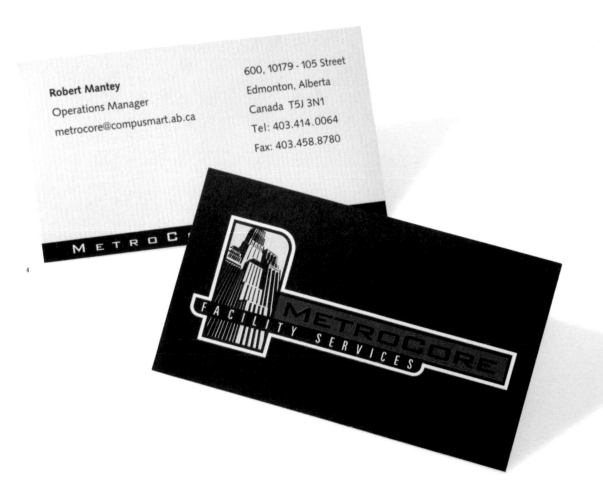

2203 First Avenue Seattle Washington 98121

p 206/ 956-RIBS (7427)

e frontierroom@seanet.com

Robert Eickhof, owner

3

FRONTIER ROOM

Robert Mantey

Operations Manager

metrocore@compusmart.ab.ca

600, 10179 - 105 Street

Edmonton, Alberta

Canada T5J 3N1

Tel: 403.414.0064

Fax: 403.458.8780

METROCORE

4

FACILITY SERVICES

METROCORE

	1
design firm	Gumption Design
art director	Evelyn Lontok Capistrano
designer	Evelyn Lontok Capistrano
client	Gumption Design
software/hardware	Adobe Illustrator, QuarkXPress
paper/materials	Carolina coated
printing	Alexander Scott Graphics

	2
design firm	Code Design Studio
art directors	Scott Bowker, Scott Toth
designers	Scott Bowker, Scott Toth
illustrators	Scott Bowker (logo), Scott Toth (font)
client	Code Design Studio
software/hardware	Adobe Illustrator, Macromedia Freehand
paper/materials	McCoy Silk 100 lb.
printing	3-color offset

raven rock media

3

morgan reese || | PRODUCER

110 old stone hill road, pound ridge, n.y. 10576
914.764.0662 || fax 914.764.0227
morgan@ravenrockmedia.com
www.ravenrockmedia.com

design firm	Leibow Studios
art director	Paul Leibow
designer	Paul Leibow
client	Raven Rock Media
software/hardware	Adobe Illustrator, QuarkXPress, Mac G3
paper/materials	Wausau Royal Fiber cottonwood 80 lb. cover
printing	Print Solutions, distributor

4

design firm	Emery Vincent Design
art director	Emery Vincent Design
designer	Emery Vincent Design
client	Commercial Television Australia (CTVA)
software/hardware	Adobe Illustrator, Mac
paper/materials	Splendargel white 30 gsm
printing	Mutual Printing

DAVID FOLEY
ASSISTANT DIRECTOR
OF ENGINEERING

CTVA
COMMERCIAL TELEVISION AUSTRALIA

44 AVENUE ROAD
MOSMAN
NSW 2088
AUSTRALIA

T 61 2 9960 2622
F 61 2 9969 3520
M 0419 602 627
E dfoley@ctva.com.au

1

CUSTOM FURNISHINGS AND ENVIRONMENTS
AT THE INTERSECTION OF ART AND LIFE

2

1	
design firm	Aloha Printing
illustrator	Jim Picquelle
client	Millennium Salon Systems
software/hardware	CorelDraw
paper/materials	80 lb. gloss cover
printing	4-color process with foil stamp on front, black back with silk lamination

2	
design firm	Matter
art directors	Rick Griffith, Jason C. Otero
client	Juno Works
software/hardware	Adobe Illustrator, Adobe Photoshop, QuarkXPress
printing	2-color offset

DEVON WELLER Director of Emerging Technologies
1701 CHURCH STREET NASHVILLE TN 37203 PHO: 615.320.1444 FAX: 615.320.0750
E MAIL: DWELLER@WHISTLERS.COM

WHISTLER'S ENTERTAINMENT GROUP

WHISTLER'S MUSIC

I.V. RECORDS

WHISTLER'S MUSIC PUBLISHING

3

design firm	Lewis Communications/Nashville
art director	Robert Froedge
designer	Robert Froedge
client	Whistler's Entertainment Group
software/hardware	Adobe Illustrator, QuarkXPress
paper/materials	Classic Crest solar white
printing	2 color/2 sides plus holes punched, by client, depending on division

4

design firm	Duck Soup Graphics, Inc.
art director	Bill Doucette
designer	Bill Doucette
client	Duck Soup Graphics, Inc.
software/hardware	Adobe Illustrator, QuarkXPress
printing	2-color match

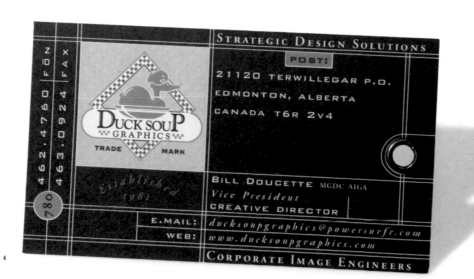

STRATEGIC DESIGN SOLUTIONS

PHONE 462.4760 FAX 463.0924

780

POST:
21120 TERWILLEGAR P.O.
EDMONTON, ALBERTA
CANADA T6R 2V4

DUCK SOUP GRAPHICS TRADE MARK

Established 1981

BILL DOUCETTE MGDC AIGA
Vice President
CREATIVE DIRECTOR

E.MAIL: ducksoupgraphics@powersurfr.com
WEB: www.ducksoupgraphics.com

CORPORATE IMAGE ENGINEERS

4

BRYN
PATRIC BEAR SALON
BRYN@CABLESPEED.COM
SALON ⤫ 206.325.6565
CALL FOR APPOINTMENT

bryn

CEL 206.719.2042

1

design firm	Design Alchemy
designer	Ole Sørensen
illustrator	Ole Sørensen
client	Bryn-Patric Bear Salon
software/hardware	Adobe Photoshop, Macromedia Freehand, Mac G4
paper/materials	12 pt. coated stock
printing	Pr1nt.com, 4/4 with spot metallic silver

2

design firm	plus design, inc.
art director	Karin Fickett
designer	Karin Fickett
client	Tony Rinaldo Photography
paper/materials	Monadnock Astrolite Smooth bright white 80 lb. cover
printing	Alpha Press

TONY RINALDO PHOTOGRAPHY ▶ POST OFFICE BOX 559 ▶ CONCORD

MASSACHUSETTS 01742 ▶ TEL. 617.923.9998 ▶ FAX. 617.923.8444

STORMSHIP
kia benjamin senior account
kia@stormship.com
781.391.9517 phone   781.395.9300 fax
the dyer building, 3

STORMSHIP
michael brennan principal
mike@stormship.com
781.391.9517 phone
781.395.9300 fax
the dyer building, 34 salem street, medford, ma 02155   www.stormship.com

3

STORM
STORM
design

3

design firm	Stormship Studios
art director	Anne Damphousse
designers	Anne Damphousse, Christine Gleason
client	Stormship Studios, Inc.
software/hardware	Adobe Illustrator, QuarkXPress
paper/materials	Potlatch, Mountie Matte
printing	3 PMS plus metallic, rounded corner die cut

4

design firm	Kontrapunkt D.O.O.
art director	Eduard Čehovin
designer	Eduard Čehovin
client	Čeligoj Andreja, Slovenia
software/hardware	Adobe Illustrator
printing	Offset

čeligoj:andreja
diplomirani
oblikovalec vizualnih komunikacij
041   516:760

rde   č:a

4

SpiderSoftware™
deliver content faster.

Laurie Maclachlan
Human Resources

512 - 1529 west 6th avenue
vancouver, bc canada v6j 1r1

604.637.0
fax 604.63

lmaclachlan@spidersoftware.com

toll-free 1.866.252.

1

www.SpiderSoftware.com

		1
design firm		Wow! A Branding Company
art director		Will Johnson
designer		Will Johnson
client		Spider Software
software/hardware		Adobe Illustrator, Mac G4
printing		Classic Printing

has an appointment

at

at

at

These times are reserved exclusively for you. 24 hours notice
is appreciated if you are unable to keep your appointment.

2

		2
design firm		Burgard Design
art director		Todd Burgard
designer		Todd Burgard
illustrator		Todd Burgard
client		Richard M. Berg, D.D.S.
software/hardware		Adobe Illustrator, QuarkXPress, °Mac G4
paper/materials		Neenah Classic Linen solar white 80 lb.
printing		1/1 offset, PMS 2603 purple, blind embossing

RICHARD M. BERG, DDS
GENERAL DENTISTRY
Warwick Center
54 Copperfield Circle
Lititz, PA 17543
Tel. 717-627-3113
Fax 717-627-0723
drberg@drberg.net

Richard M. Berg
Dentist

VETANA

1126 WOOD AVE | ADDISON | ILLINOIS |
P 630.773.2773 | WWW.VETANA.CO

JAMIE LAING
E JAMIE@VETANA.COM
C 773.307.2638

3

design firm	Firebelly Design Co.
art director	Dawn Hancock
designer	Dawn Hancock
client	Ventana
software/hardware	Adobe Illustrator, Mac G4
paper/materials	Mohawk Superfine Smooth 110 lb. cover
printing	2/1 offset, Ladendorf Bros.

4

design firm	Firebelly Design Co.
art director	Dawn Hancock
designer	Dawn Hancock
client	Firebelly Design Co.
software/hardware	Adobe Illustrator, Mac G4
paper/materials	Mohawk Superfine Smooth 110 lb. cover
printing	2/0 offset, Ladendorf Bros.

FIREBELLY DESIGN
GOOD DESIGN FOR GOOD REASON

DAWN HANCOCK *creative director*
DAWN@FIREBELLYDESIGN.COM

FIREBELLY DESIGN CO.
2701 WEST THOMAS AVE
CHICAGO IL 60622 USA

* P 773 489 3200
F 773 489 3439
FIREBELLYDESIGN.COM

4

design firm	RocketDog Communications
art directors	Susan Elliott, Michael Elliott
designer	Damon Nakagawa
illustrator	Greg McMurchie
client	RocketDog Communications
software/hardware	Macromedia Freehand
paper/materials	Mohawk Navajo
printing	Sheetfed offset, die cut, metallic ink, custom sleeve with blind embossing

jeff gilligan art direction+design

917.513.0569 www.jeffgilligan.com

1

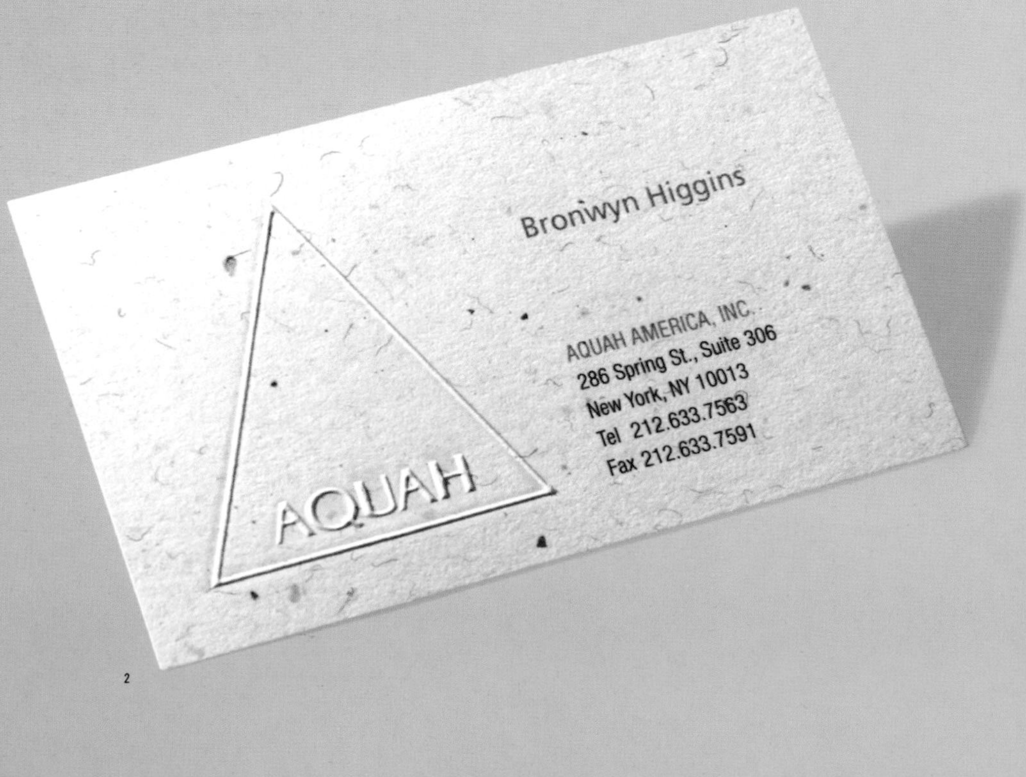

1	
design firm	Jeff Gilligan
art director	Jeff Gilligan
designer	Jeff Gilligan
client	Jeff Gilligan
software/hardware	Adobe Photoshop, QuarkXPress
printing	2/2

2	
design firm	Gatta Design & Co., Inc.
art director	Kevin Gatta
designer	Kevin Gatta
client	Aquah America, Inc.
software/hardware	Adobe Illustrator, QuarkXPress, Mac
paper/materials	Fox River Confetti
printing	Continental-Anchor Engraving, Inc.

Bronwyn Higgins

AQUAH AMERICA, INC.
286 Spring St., Suite 306
New York, NY 10013
Tel 212.633.7563
Fax 212.633.7591

AQUAH

2

3

FREED ARNOLD ARCHITECTURE

GEORGE ARNOLD

570 EAST FIRST STREET
BOSTON MA 02127
P 617 268 4302 F 617 268 4307
TWO_ARCHITECTS@JUNO.COM

3	
design firm	Nassar Design
art director	Nélida Nassar
designer	Margarita Encomienda
client	Freed Arnold Architecture
software/hardware	QuarkXPress
paper/materials	Canson Curious Silver Satin cover 58 lb.
printing	Alpha Press

4	
design firm	Morrow McKenzie Design
art director	Elizabeth Morrow McKenzie
designer	Elizabeth Morrow McKenzie
client	Kat Nyberg Photography
software/hardware	Adobe Illustrator, Adobe Photoshop, QuarkXPress
paper/materials	White uncoated 100 lb. card stock
printing	Indigo digital, 4-color process

kat nyberg
PHOTOGRAPHY INC

4

KAT NYBERG
TELEPHONE 503 349 6712
FACSIMILE 503 284 0706
4619 NE 7TH AVENUE
PORTLAND, OR 97211
KATNYBERG@MAC.COM

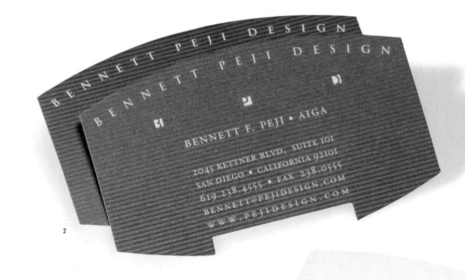

watts design

66 albert road south melbourne
victoria 3205 australia
phone 03 9696 4116
fax 03 9696 4006
mobile 0417 307 298
email peter@wattsdesign.com.au
web wattsdesign.com.au

peter watts

1

watts design

communication that's
memorable, emotive and enduring

	1
design firm	Watts Design
art directors	Peter and Helen Watts
designers	Peter and Helen Watts
client	Watts Design
software/hardware	Adobe Illustrator
paper/materials	Ever
printing	Bambra Press

BENNETT PEJI DESIGN

BENNETT PEJI DESIGN

BENNETT F. PEJI • AIGA

2045 KETTNER BLVD, SUITE 101
SAN DIEGO • CALIFORNIA 92101
619.238.4555 • FAX 238.0555
BENNETT@PEJIDESIGN.COM
WWW.PEJIDESIGN.COM

2

	2
design firm	Bennett Peji Design
art director	Bennett Peji
designers	Bennett, Peji, Nicholas Inzunza
illustrator	Bennett Peji
client	Bennett Peji Design
software/hardware	Adobe Illustrator, Mac G4
paper/materials	Smart Papers, Benefit, In to Ink

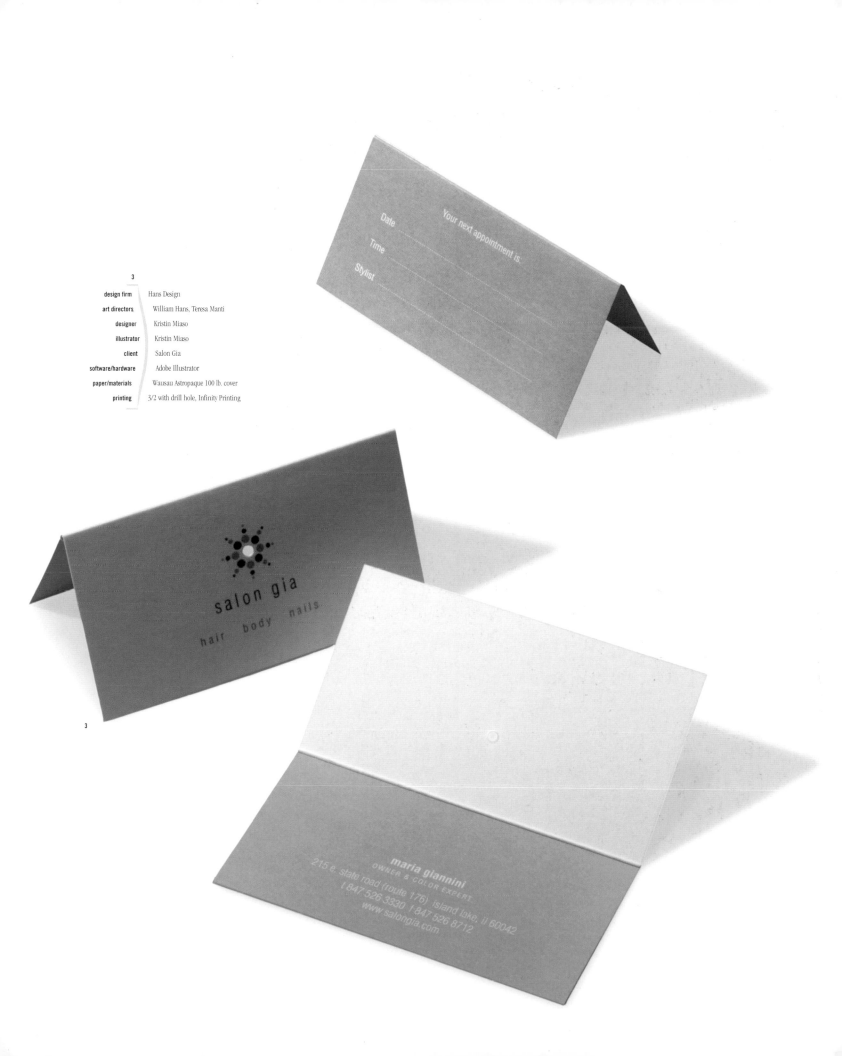

3	
design firm	Hans Design
art directors	William Hans, Teresa Manti
designer	Kristin Miaso
illustrator	Kristin Miaso
client	Salon Gia
software/hardware	Adobe Illustrator
paper/materials	Wausau Astropaque 100 lb. cover
printing	3/2 with drill hole, Infinity Printing

Your next appointment is:

Date

Time

Stylist

salon gia
hair   body   nails.

maria giannini
OWNER & COLOR EXPERT.
215 e. state road (route 176) island lake, il 60042
t 847 526 3930 f 847 526 8712
www.salongia.com

3

design firm	Scott Love Design
designer	Scott Love
client	Scott Goodwin Photography
software/hardware	Adobe Illustrator
paper/materials	Nickel Silver
printing	Etching

Frauke Willems PR

Oderfelderstrasse 21   20149 Hamburg   Telefon +49 (0)40 - 47 77 92
Telefax +49 (0)40 - 460 07 986   frauke-willems@hamburg.de

1

⚹

kim meyers warren
ASLA

p.o. box 1096
boise, id 83701
208/841.0914
kmeyerswarren@msn.com

2

1	
design firm	Marius Fahrner Design
art director	Marius Fahrner
designer	Marius Fahrner
illustrator	Marius Fahrner
client	Frauke Williems Public Relations
software/hardware	Macromedia Freehand
printing	1-color metallic gray

2	
design firm	Kristy Weyhrich
art director	Kristy Weyhrich
designer	Kristy Weyhrich
client	Kim Meyers Warren
software/hardware	Adobe Illustrator, Mac
paper/materials	French Frostone
printing	Letterpress, Full Circle Press

CERTIFIED
MASSAGE THERAPIST

Andrea Kocerha

215 991 4701 | AKOCERHA@EARTHLINK.NET

BY APPOINTMENT   HOURLY RATES   STARVING ARTIST RATES

3

logolounge.com

Cathy Fishel

cathy@logolounge.com

515 East Madison Street | Morton, Illinois USA 61550

T 309 / 266 / 9299 | 309 / 263 / 8622 F

4

design firm	Tracy Design
art director	Jan Tracy
designer	Patrick Simone
client	Jennifer Anne LLC
software/hardware	Adobe Illustrator
paper/materials	Curious metallic ice cold
printing	2-color offset

jenniferanne LLC.

1

business contact / +6
email / alena@indo.n
fax / +62 21 580 49

alena

alena

alena

alena

business contact / +62 (0) 8131 061 3937
email / alena@indo.net.id
fax / +62 21 580 4906

1

design firm	MiD
designer	Michelle S. Zacharia
client	Alena
software/hardware	Adobe Illustrator, Adobe Photoshop
paper/materials	Superfine 300 gsm
printing	4 color plus 2 special metallic colors

FM Organics

PO Box 22 Endeavour Hills Victoria 3802
T 613 9700 7352
F 613 9700 7198 M 0412 731 851
E pod.fmorganics@iprimus.com.au

pod

2

Youssef Fares Managing Director

pod

2

design firm	Watts Design
art directors	Peter and Helen Watts
designer	David Fry
client	Pod Organics

être

être
your capital, your vision

3

design firm	plus design, inc.
art director	Anita Meyer
designers	Anita Meyer, Amada Poray
client	être llc
paper/materials	Business card: Crane's Crest florescent white wove 110 lb. cover
	Envelope: Crane's Crest florescent white wove 28 lb. cover
printing	The Artcraft Company, Inc.

paula e chauncey cfa | pchauncey@etrellc.com

être llc

300 boylston street suite 909 | boston massachusetts 02116
voice 617.357.7385 | **fax** 617.536.6967 www.etrellc.com

design firm	ARTiculation Group
art director	Joseph Chan
designer	Joseph Chan
illustrator	Joseph Chan
client	Dr. Angela C. S. Tam
software/hardware	Adobe Illustrator, Mac G3, G4
paper/materials	Strathmore
printing	Offset

YOUR NEXT APPOINTMENT.

at

at

at

at

IF YOU ARE UNABLE TO KEEP THIS APPOINTMENT,
PLEASE NOTIFY US 24 HOURS IN ADVANCE, IN WHICH
CASE NO CHARGE WILL BE MADE.

Hwy 7

維雅廣場

Steeles Av. W.

DR. ANGELA C. S. TAM 牙醫譚誦詩

DENTAL SURGEON

7368 YONGE STREET, SUITE 108
THORNHILL, ONTARIO L4J 8H9
TEL 905.889.5723 · FAX 905.889.5240

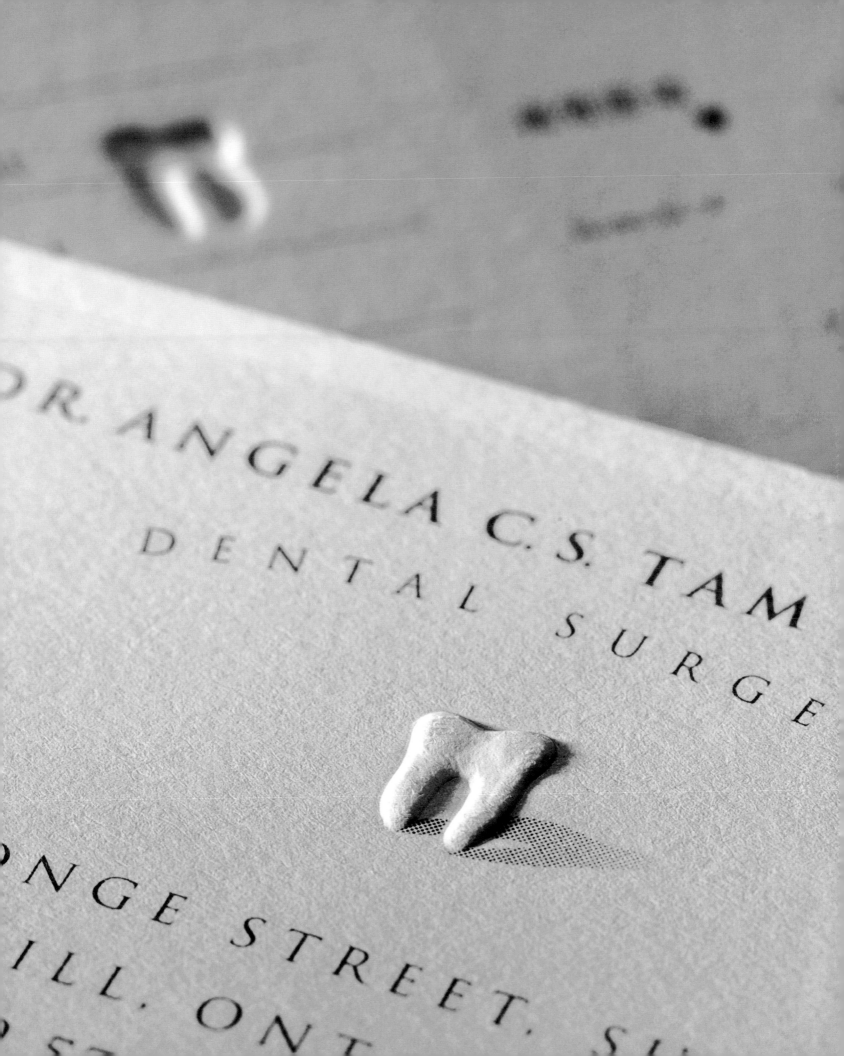

DR. ANGELA C.S. TAM
DENTAL SURGE

NGE STREET, S
ILL, ONT

1

> Design + Visual Communications

MONDERER DESIGN

2067 Massachusetts Avenue
Cambridge, MA 02140-1337
617 661 6125 FAX 661 6126
www.monderer.com

	1
design firm	Monderer Design
art director	Stewart Monderer
designer	Jason Miller
client	Monderer Design
software/hardware	Adobe Illustrator, QuarkXPress
paper/materials	Astrolite 120 lb. cover

advertising**management**services

robin harris
rharris@advertisingmanagement.com
283 south main street
andover, massachusetts 01810

voice
978 475 6239

fax
978 470 1864

web
advertisingmanagement.com

	2
design firm	David Salafia
art director	David Salafia
designer	David Salafia
client	Advertising Management Services, Inc.
software/hardware	QuarkXPress
paper/materials	Gilbert Realm
printing	Arlington Lithograph

2

3

design firm	Design Alchemy
designer	Ole Sørensen
illustrator	Ole Sørensen
client	Respect Recordings
software/hardware	Adobe Photoshop, Macromedia Freehand, Mac G4
paper/materials	Microlaminated 12 pt. coated stock
printing	Pr1nt.com

4

design firm	Firebox Media
art director	Audrey Feely
client	Daga Architects
software/hardware	Adobe Illustrator
paper/materials	Strathmore
printing	Pantone

URBAN HABITAT

JULIET ELLIS
EXECUTIVE DIRECTOR

436 14TH STREET, STE 1205
OAKLAND, CA 94612
T 510 839 9512 F 510 839 9610
jre@urbanhabitat.org
www.urbanhabitat.org

1

1	
design firm	Tom & John: A Design Collaborative
art director	Tom Sizu
designer	Tom Sizu
client	Urban Habitat
software/hardware	Adobe Illustrator, Mac
paper/materials	Watercolor, Classic Crest
printing	Letterpress

2	
design firm	Wow! A Branding Company
art director	Perry Chua
designer	Will Johnson
client	Accupro Trademark Services
software/hardware	Adobe Illustrator, Mac G4
printing	Generation Printing

2

3	
design firm	Rule 29
art directors	Justin Ahrens, Jim Boborci
designers	Justin Ahrens, Jom Borborci, Jon McGrath
client	Mindware Creative
software/hardware	Adobe Illustrator, QuarkXPress
paper/materials	Nekoosa Solutions Smooth carrera white 100 lb. cover
printing	O'Neil Printing

4	
design firm	Moore Graphic Design
art director	Michele Moore
designer	Michele Moore
client	Moore Graphic Design
software/hardware	Adobe Illustrator, Mac G4
paper/materials	McCoy Silk 120 lb. cover
printing	David Mayes

3

www.mindware1.com

mindware

EVERETT L. BUTLER

3115 NORTH WILKE ROAD, SUITE S
ARLINGTON HEIGHTS, IL 60004

P 847 577 7491 x107
F 847 577 7492
E ebutler@mindware1.com

4

mgd

moore graphic design
los angeles ca 90036
323.623.6603 > phone/fax
mooregraphicdesign.com

Simon Asher

inventri

GPO Box 4769
Melbourne 3001 Australia
Mobile 0417 067 247
simon.asher@inventri.com
www.inventri.com

1	
design firm	Octavo Design
art director	Gary Domoney
client	Inventri
software/hardware	Adobe Illustrator, Mac
paper/materials	White A art board 360 gsm
printing	4 PMS colors both sides, matte film lamination and spot UV varnish both sides

2	
design firm	Kolegram Design
art director	Mike Teixeira
designer	Mike Teixeira
illustrator	Mike Teixeira
client	Intertech
software/hardware	Adobe Illustrator, QuarkXPress
paper/materials	Horizon Dull

inter.tech´
AMEUBLEMENTS DE BUREAU

PLANIFICATION
CRÉATION
CONSULTATION
ÉBÉNISTERIE
ÉVALUATION
REHOUSSAGE
REPOLISSAGE
INSTALLATION

Liette Parent
Vice-présidente

8130, boul. décarie ● montréal (qc) ● h4p 2s8 ● lparent@ca.inter.net ● téléc. / 514.344.3391
tél. / 514.344.2333 www.intertechip.com

Tony Nguyen
tony@firebladestudio.com

2997 cohansey drive
san jose, ca 95132

408 668 0536

3	
design firm	Fireblade Studio
art director	Tony Nguyen
designer	Tony Nguyen
client	Fireblade Studio
software/hardware	Adobe Illustrator
paper/materials	Tiarra Starwhite 110 lb. cover
printing	Hillis Printing

JECO POWER
DEVELOPMENTS

JESSE NEUFIELD
President
Email: jecopower@hotmail.com

P.O. Box 1493, STN. MAIN, Edmonton, Alberta T5J 2N7
Telephone: 780.482.5323 Telefax: 780.455.7420
Tollfree: 1.866.532.6562 (1.866.JecoJob)

4	
design firm	Duck Soup Graphics, Inc.
art director	Bill Doucette
designer	Bill Doucette
client	Jeco Power Developments
software/hardware	Adobe Illustrator
paper/materials	Synergy
printing	2 color, embossing

enjoy

Accord
INSURANCE BROKERS

we'll leap tall buildings

Phil Sowman

Accord Insurance Brokers
Blenheim | 276 Old Renwick Road | Tel 03 577 5522 | Fax 03 577 5563
Wellington | Box 45, Wellington | Tel 04 471 1649 | Fax 04 471 1451
Mobile 025 464 475 Email: phil@accordbrokers.co.nz

Accord
INSURANCE BROKERS

look before you leap

Phil Sowman

Accord Insurance Brokers
Blenheim | 276 Old Renwick Road | Tel 03 577 5522 | Fax 03 577 5563
Wellington | Box 45, Wellington | Tel 04 471 1649 | Fax 04 471 1451
Mobile 025 464 475 Email: phil@accordbrokers.co.nz

different

design firm	Lloyds Graphic Design & Communication
art director	Alexander Lloyd
designer	Alexander Lloyd
client	HavanaStreet.com/Toby Lloyd
software/hardware	Adobe Photoshop, Macromedia Freehand, Mac G4
paper/materials	Matte art board 220 gsm
printing	Offset

directory

A

Laurie Schiada
Accentuate Inc.
15320 Cornet Ave.
Santa Fe Springs, CA 90670 USA
Phone: (562) 404-4976
Fax: (562) 921-7038
lschiada@accentuateinc.com
{177}

Russ Haan
After Hours Creative
5444 E. Washington, Ste. 3
Phoenix, AZ 85034 USA
Phone: (602) 275-5200
Fax: (602) 275-5700
{145}

Lans Brahmantyo
Afterhours Group
Jalan Merpati Raya 45
Menteng Dalam Jakarta 12870
Indonesia
Phone: +62 21 8306819
Fax: +62 21 8290612
brahm@afterhoursgroup.com
{178}

Jim Piquelle
Aloha Printing
880 W. 19th St.
Costa Mesa, CA 92627 USA
Phone: (949) 722-6761
Fax: (949) 642-7058
alohaprinting@attbi.com
{192}

Anastasia Design
249 Newbury St.
Boston, MA 02116 USA
Phone: (617) 262-1515
Fax: (617) 262-1919
anastasia@anastasiadesign.com
{90}

Anders Malmströmer
Anders Malmströmer Grafisk Design
Stora Nygatan 7
Stockholm SE-111 27
Sweden
Phone: +46 (0) 8-677 00 84
Fax: +46 (0) 8 677 00 98
a.malmstromer@telia.com
{31}

Alan Ratliff
Anvil Graphic Design, Inc.
2611 Broadway
Redwood City, CA 94063 USA
Phone: (650) 261-6095
Fax: (650) 261-6094
aratliff@hitanvil.com
{59}

Joseph Chan
ARTiculation Group
33 Bloor St. E., 13/F, Ste. 1302
Toronto, ON M4W 3T4
Canada
Phone: (416) 922-7999
Fax: (416) 922-1683
{46–47,150–151, 212–213}

John O'Brien
Artministry, Inc.
5211 Kester, Ste. 201
Sherman Oaks, CA 91411 USA
{104}

B

Todd Goodman
Bandujo Donker & Brothers
396 Springfield Ave.
Summit, NJ 07901 USA
Phone: (908) 608-2032
Fax: (908) 608-2030
tgoodman@bandujo.com
{170}

Barbara and Gerd Baumann
Baumann & Baumann
Taubentalstr. 411
73525 Schwäbisch Gmünd
Germany
Phone: 0049 7171 927990
Fax: 0049 7171 927999
info@baumannandbaumann.com
{120, 122, 180–181}

Shinichi Eguchi
Be.Design
1306 Third St.
San Rafael, CA 94901 USA
Phone: (415) 451-3530
Fax: (415) 451-3532
shinichi_eguchi@beplanet.com
{14}

Bennett Peji
Bennett Peji Design
2802 W. Canyon Ave.
San Diego, CA 92123 USA
Phone: (858) 874-8514
bennett@pejidesign.com
{176, 202}

Blackcoffee™
840 Summer Street
Boston, MA 02127 USA
Phone: (617) 268-1116
info@blackcoffee.com
{8–13}

Christine Dzieciolowski
Blank, Inc.
1878 Monroe St., NW
Washington, DC 20010 USA
Phone: (202) 319-3120
Fax: (202) 319-8930
christined@blankblank.com
{30, 108, 187}

Ali Filsoof
Bluespark Studios
1335 4th St., #201
Santa Monica, CA 90401 USA
Phone: (310) 394-9080
Fax: (310) 394-9588
ali@bluesparkstudios.com
{22, 45, 108}

Dian Sourelis
Brainforest, Inc.
1735 N. Paulina, #409
Chicago, IL 60622 USA
Phone: (773) 395-2500
dian@brainforest.com
{54, 103, 155, 167}

Carlos Coeiho
Brandia Network
Edificio Goncalves Zarco
Doca de Alcantara 1350-352
Lisbon, Portgual
Phone: 00351 213923000
Fax: 00351 213953849
carloscoeiho@novodesign.pt
{26–27}

Todd Burgard
Burgard Design
342 Walnut St.
Columbia, PA 17512 USA
Phone: (717) 684-5896
Fax: (717) 684-5896
gideon@redrose.net
{196}

Patrick Burgeff
Burgeff Co.
Tecualiapan 36 V11/8
Mexico City 04320
Mexico
Phone: +52 55545931
Fax: +52 55545931
pburgeff@hotmail.com
{105}

C
Cherish Reynoso
Campbell Fisher Design
3333 E. Camelback Rd., Ste. 200
Phoenix, AZ 85018 USA
Phone: (602) 955-2707
Fax: (602) 955-2878
mail@cfd2k.com
cr@cfd2k.com
{30, 35, 48, 55, 102, 107}

Ira Payer
Cavarpayer
Berislaviceva 14
Zagreb 10000
Croatia
Phone: +385 1 4872 420
Fax: +385 1 4872427
studio@cavarpayer.com
{112–113}

Joshua Chen
Chen Design Associates
589 Howard St.
San Francisco, CA 94105 USA
Phone: (415) 896-5338
Fax: (415) 896-5339
info@chendesign.com
{35, 184}

Dusty Sumner
CHRW Advertising
106 W. 11th St., Ste. 2220
Kansas City, MO 64105 USA
Phone: (816) 472-4455
Fax: (816) 472-8855
dusty@chrwadvertising.com
{48}

Scott Bowker
Code Design Studio
7251 Browning Rd.
Pennsauken, NJ 08109 USA
Phone: (856) 486-9106
Fax: (856) 486-9618
sbowker@codeds.com
{190}

Renée Sallee
Code Red Design
17821 Lassen St., #129
Northridge, CA 91325 USA
Phone: (818) 634-9908
Fax: (818) 885-7669
renee@codered-design.com
{101}

James Evelock
Collaborated, Inc.
179 Boylston St.
Jamaica Plain, MA 02130 USA
Phone: (617) 983-0500
james@collaboratedinc.com
{21,173, 207}

Dianne O'Hehir
CPd
333 Funders Lane, 2nd floor
Melbourne, Victoria 3000
Australia
Phone: +61 39620 5911
Fax: +61 39620 5922
d.ohehir@cpdtotal.com.au
{161, 171}

D
Wicky Lee
D4 Creative Group
161 Leverington Ave., Ste. 1001
Philadelphia, PA 19127 USA
Phone: (215) 483-4555
Fax: (215) 483-4554
lee@d4creative.com
{16, 85}

Damion Hickman
Damion Hickman Design
1801 Dove, #104
Newport Beach, CA 92660 USA
Phone: (949) 261-7857
damion@damionhickman.com
{140}

Dan Elliott
36 Rythe Court, Portsmouth Rd.
Thames Ditton, Surrey KT7 CTE
UK
Phone: +0207420 7728
daniele@wilsonharvey.co.uk
{135, 186, 188}

Dara Turransky
Dara Turransky Design
12801 66th Ave., SE
Snohomish, WA 98296 USA
Phone: (425) 337-6634
Fax: (425) 337-6634
dara@turransky.com
{38}

David Clark
David Clark Design
1305 E. 15th St., Ste. 202
Tulsa, OK 74120 USA
Phone: (918) 295-0044
Fax: (918) 295-0055
dc@tulsaconnect.com
{140}

David Salafia
56R Whittier St.
Andover, MA 01810 USA
Phone: (978) 409-1300
ds@pangardbeer.com
{214}

Gareth Debenham
Debenham Design, Inc.
200 Highland Ave., 2nd floor
Needham, MA 02494 USA
Phone: (781) 444-8515
Fax: (781) 444-8560
gareth@debenhamdesign.com
{28, 127, 171}

Ron Nikkel
Design 5
7636 N. Ingram, 102
Fresno, CA 93711 USA
Phone: (559) 432-5110
Fax: (559) 432-6158
info@designfive.com
{172}

Ole sørensen
Design Alchemy
1122 E. Pike St., #921
Seattle, WA 98122 USA
Phone: (206) 227-1022
designalchemy@mac.com
{93, 129, 134, 194, 215}

Lauren Chan
Detroit Creative
165 1020 Mainland St.,
Vancouver, BC V6B 2T4
Canada
Phone: (604) 408-7040
Fax: (604) 408 7041
lchan@detroit.ca
{80}

Dallas Drotz
Drotz Design
1613 12th Ave., SW
Puyallup, WA 98371 USA
Phone: (253) 678-2156
info@drotzdesign.com
{132}

Bill Doucette
Duck Soup Graphics, Inc.
464 Butchart Dr.
Edmonton, AB T6R 2N8
Canada
Phone: (780) 462-4760
Fax: (780) 462-0924
ducksoupgraphics@shawbiz.ca
{28, 90, 189, 193, 219}

Michelle Tan
Duffy Singapore
25 Duxton Hill 089608
Singapore
Phone: +65 6324 7827
Fax: +65 6324 8265
michelle.tan@duffy.com
{118, 182–183}

E
Sharon Nixon
Emery Vincent Design
Level 1, 15 Foster St.
Surry Hills, NSW 2010
Australia
Phone: +61 2 9280 4233
Fax: +61 2 9280 4266
sharon.nixon@evd.com.au
{23, 191}

Emma Wilson
Emma Wilson Design Co.
500 Aurora Avenue N.
Seattle, WA 98109
{189}

Leslie Guidice
Energy Energy Design
246 Blossom Hill Rd.
Los Gatos, CA 95032 USA
Phone: (408) 395-5911
Fax: (408) 395-8285
leslieg@nrgdesign.com
{45, 55}

Brian Cartwright
Entermotion Design Studio
106 S. Emporia
Wichita, KS 67202 USA
Phone: (316) 264-2277
brian@entermotion.com
{41, 186}

F
Dawn Hancock
Firebelly Design Co.
2701 W. Thomas, 2nd floor
Chicago, IL 60622 USA
Phone: (773) 489-3200
Fax: (773) 489-3439
info@firebellydesign.com
{84, 187, 197}

Tony Nguyen
Fireblade Studio
2997 Cohansey Dr.
San Jose, CA 95132 USA
Phone: (408) 666-0536
tony@firebladestudio.com
{219}

Audrey Feely
Firebox Media
569 Waller St.
San Francisco, CA 94117 USA
Phone: (415) 436-9997
Fax: (415) 358-5637
audrey@fireboxmedia.com
{215}

Lisa Nankervis
Flight Creative
Studio 14, 15 Inkerman St.
St. Kilda, Victoria 3182
Australia
Phone: +61 3 9534 4690
Fax: +61 3 9593 6029
mail@flightcreative.com
{73}

Kelly Andrus
Forma Design
715 Tucker St.
Raleigh, NC 27603 USA
Phone: (919) 832-1244
Fax: (919) 832-4522
kandrus@forma-design.com
{135, 153}

Daniel Bastian
Form Fuenf Bremen
Graf Moltke Str. 7
28203 Bremen
Germany
Phone: +49 421 703074
Fax: +49 421 703740
bastian@form5.de
{141, 146}

Jeff Culver
Function
7929 Greelake Dr., N., #22
Seattle, WA 98103 USA
Phone: (206) 523-7287
jeffc@functionco.com
{102, 184}

G

Elisabeth Ryherd
Gardner Design
3204 E. Douglas
Wichita, KS 67208 USA
Phone: (316) 691-8808
Fax: (316) 691-8818
elisabeth@gardnerdesign.net
{31, 32, 65, 77, 111, 126, 149, 159, 166, 178, 207}

Danielle Winfield
Gateway Arts
810 Lawrence Dr., #220
Thousand Oaks, CA 91320 USA
Phone: (805) 480-1140 ext. 226
Fax: (805) 480-1150
danielle@gatewayarts.com
{104, 177}

Kevin Gatta
Gatta Design & Co., Inc.
286 Spring St., Ste. 301
New York, NY 10013 USA
Phone: (212) 229-0071
Fax: (212) 229-0074
mail@gattago.com
{200}

Jeff MacFarlane
Get Smart Design Co.
899 Jackson St.
Dubuque, IA 52001-7014 USA
Phone: (563) 583-0853
Fax: (563) 583-0664
jeff@getsmartdesign.com
{172}

Fabian Geyrhalter
Geyrhalter Design
6751/2 Rose Ave.
Venice, CA 90291 USA
Phone: (310) 392-7615
Fax: (310) 392-7615
fabian@geyrhalter.com
{86–87}

Von R. Glitschka
Glitschka Studios
5165 Sycan Ct., SE
Salem, OR 97306 USA
Phone: (503) 581-5340
Fax: (503) 585-8190
von@glitschka.com
{160}

Diane Shaw
Goodesign
4 W. 37th St., #5
New York, NY 10018 USA
Phone: (646) 473-1520
Fax: (646) 473-1519
diane@goodesignny.com
{116, 117, 156}

Jonanthan Gouthier
Gouthier Design, Inc.
2604 NW 54th St.
Fort Lauderdale, FL 33309 USA
Phone: (954) 739-7430
Fax: (954) 739-3746
jon@gouthier.com
{96, 97}

Marius Ursache
Grapefruit Design
Str. Garii 5, Bl. L17, Ap. 1
Iasi, IS 700094
Romania
Phone: +40 744 863740
Fax: +40 232 233068
office@grapefruitdesign.com
www.grapefruitdesign.com
{167}

Herbert Rohsiepe
graphische formgebung
Pulverstrasse 25
Bochum 44869
Germany
Phone: +49 23 27 95 76 21
Fax: +49 23 27 95 76 22
herbert.rohsiepe@gelsen.net
{92}

Evelyn Lontok Capistrano
Gumption Design
24 Scott Alley
San Francisco, CA 94107 USA
Phone: (415) 979-9290
Fax: (415) 979-9291
evelyn@gumptiondesign.com
{190}

H

Bob Hambly
Hambly & Woolley, Inc.
130 Spadina Ave., #807
Toronto, ON M5V 2L4
Canada
Phone: (416) 504-2742
Fax: (416) 504-2745
bobh@hamblywoolley.com
{14, 18, 91, 111, 136}

Alessandro Esteri
Hand Made Group
Via Sartori, No. 16
Stia, Arezzo 52017
Italy
Phone: +0575 582083
Fax: +0575 582198
info@hmg.it
{36}

William Hans
Hans Design
3100 Dundee Rd., Ste. 909
Northbrook, IL 60062 USA
Phone: (847) 272-7980
Fax: (847) 272-8006
kristin@hansdesign.com
bill@hansdesign.com
{203}

I

Nessim Higson
iamalwayshungry
4001 Leeword Ave.
Los Angeles, CA 90005 USA
Phone: (205) 401-8001
ness@iamalwayshungry.com
{14, 164}

Marcie Carson
IE Design
1600 Rosecrans Ave., Bld. 6B, #200
Manhattan Beach, CA 90266 USA
Phone: (310) 727-3500
Fax: (310) 727-3515
marcie@iedesign.net
{41, 75, 81}

Andreas Kranz
impraxis, raum für gestaltung
Orleansstrasse 5
Munich 81669
Germany
Phone: +49 89 444 39860
Fax: +49 89 444 39880
kontakt@inpraxis.com
{33, 34}

Harvey Appelbaum
Inc-3
220 E. 23rd St.
New York, NY 10010 USA
Phone: (212) 213-1130
Fax: (212) 532-8022
happel@inc-3.com
{121}

Jennifer Won
Inkspot
20 Vernon St., 5th floor
Somerville, MA 02143 USA
Phone: (617) 653-4647
info@inkspot-press.com
{74}

Doug Logan
Inovat Design
544 Mark Dr.
Elizabethtown, PA 17022-9405 USA
Phone: (717) 367-5446
Fax: (717) 367-7180
doug@inovat.com
{51}

Mark D. Sylvester
**Interrobang Design
Collaborative, Inc.**
2385 Huntington Rd.
Richmond, VT 05477 USA
Phone: (802) 434-5970
Fax: (802) 434-6313
mark@interrobangdesign.com
{60–61}

Mario L'Ecuyer
iridium, a design agency
43 Eccles St., 2nd floor
Ottawa, ON K1R 6S3
Canada
Phone: (613) 748-3336
Fax: (613) 748-3372
ideas@irium192.com
{56, 81, 82}

J
Jeff Fisher
Jeff Fisher LogoMotives
P.O. Box 17155
Portland, OR 97217 USA
Phone: (503) 283-8673
Fax: (503) 283-8995
jeff@jfisherlogomotives.com
{39}

Jeff Gilligan
Jeff Gilligan Art and Direction
655 E. 14th St., Apt. 9C
New York, NY 10009 USA
Phone: (917) 513-0569
info@jeffgilligan.com
{200}

john Kneapler
John Kneapler Design
151 W. 19th St., #11C
New York, NY 10011 USA
Phone: (212) 463-9774
Fax: (212) 463-0478
jkneapler@aol.com
{21, 40}

Justin Skeesuck
Justin Skeesuck Design Studio
7630 Marie Ave.
La Mesa, CA 91941 USA
Phone: (619) 277-2585
jskeez@cox.net
{143}

K
Kerry Harrington
karacters design group
1600-777 Hornby St.
Vancouver, BC V6Z 2T3
Canada
Phone: (604) 609-9508
kerry.harrington@karacters.com
{72}

Terri Fry Kasuba
Kasuba Design Company
40 E. Benedict Ave.
Havertown, PA 19083 USA
Phone: (610) 754-2249
Fax: (610) 789-9352
terri@kasubadesign.com
{127}

Kelly McMurray
Kellydesign, Inc.
1208 Massachusetts Ave., Ste. 7
Cambridge, MA 02138 USA
Phone: (617) 868-3500
Fax: (617) 868-3501
kelly@kellydesigninc.com
{75, 176}

Kevin Foley
KF Design
Takazeki-Machi 385 #401
Takasaki, Gunma 370-0043
Japan
Phone: +81 27 320 8300
Fax: +81 27 320 8301
kevin@kfdesign.jp
{142}

Jenny Stillman
Kinetik
1436 U St. NW, Ste. 404
Washington, DC 20009 USA
Phone: (202) 797-0605
Fax: (202) 797-2848
sam@kinetikcom.com
{66–67, 117}

Mike Teixeira
Kolegram Design
37 boul. St. Joseph
Hull, QC J8Y 3V8
Canada
Phone: (819) 777-5538
Fax: (819) 777-8525
mike@kolegram.com
{100, 114, 139, 165, 218}

Eduard Čehovin
Kontrapunkt D.O.O.
Parmova 20
Ljubljana 1000
Slovenia
Phone: 386 (1) 519 5072
Fax: 386 (1) 519 5072
eduard.cehovin@siol.net
{78, 157, 195}

Jill Vartenigian
Momentum Press and Design
13546 36th Ave., NE
Seattle, WA 98125 USA
Phone: (206) 390-0232
Fax: (206) 417-1821
hill@momentumpress.com
{106, 154}

Stewart Monderer
Monderer Design
2067 Massachusetts Ave.
Cambridge, MA 02140 USA
Phone: (617) 661-6125
Fax: (617) 661-6126
stewart@monderer.com
{214}

Denise Sakaki
Monster Design
7816 Leary Way NE, #200
Redmond, WA 98052 USA
Phone: (425) 828-7853
Fax: (425) 576-8055
info@monsterinvasion.com
{38, 96, 101, 157}

Michele Moore
Moore Graphic Design
338 N. Genesee Ave.
Los Angeles, CA 90036 USA
Phone: (323) 936-6603
Fax: (323) 936-6603
mcm@michelecomas.com
{217}

Elizabeth Morrow McKenzie
Morrow McKenzie Design
322 NW 5th Ave., Ste. 313
Portland, OR 97209 USA
Phone: (503) 222-0331
Fax: (503) 296-2332
elizabeth@morrowmckenzie.com
{79, 201}

Perry Chua
Move Creative
2468 E. Broadway
Vancouver, BC V5M 4V1
Canada
Phone: (604) 809-1778
perry@movecreative.ca
{115}

N
Alicia Martínez Díaz
91nueveuno
c/Infantas, 15-30 izda
Madrid 28004
Spain
Phone: +34 91 521 66 84
alicia@nueveuno.com
{121}

Nélida Nassar
Nassar Design
11 Park St.
Brookline, MA 02446 USA
Phone: (617) 264-2862
Fax: (617) 264-2861
n.nassar@verizon.net
{118, 130, 137, 165, 201}

Nelia Vishnevsky
65 St. Marks Pl., #2
New York, NY 10003 USA
Phone: (212) 254-3782; (917) 751-6640
nvishnevsky@yahoo.com
{44}

Maria Bez
Northbank
16 Gay St.
Bath BAI 2PH
UK
Phone: +01225 332703
{52, 133}

O
Tim Oakley
Oakley Design Studios
519 SW Park Ave., #210
Portland, OR 97205 USA
Phone: (503) 241-3705
oakleyds@oakleydesign.com
{98–99}

Lee Felch
Octane
720 Tahoe St., #1
Reno, NV 89509 USA
Phone: (775) 323-7887
Fax: (775) 323-4187
jim@octanestudios.com
{49}

Gary Domoney
Octavo Design Pty. Ltd.
130 Kerr St.
Fitzroy, Victoria 3065
Australia
Phone: +613 9417 6022
Fax: +613 9417 6255
info@octavedesign.com.au
{37, 44, 71, 89, 161, 218}

Kristy Weyhrich
Oliver Russell
217 S. 11th
Boise, ID 83702 USA
Phone: (208) 344-1734
Fax: (208) 344-1211
weyhrich@oh-zone.com
{40}

Damien Wolf
OrangeSeed Design
800 Washington Ave., N., Ste. 461
Minneapolis, MN 55401 USA
Phone: (612) 252-9757
Fax: (612) 252-9760
dwolf@orangeseed.com
{115}

P
Jason Hill
Papercut Interactive, Inc.
119 E. Meadowbrook Dr.
Chattanooga, TN 37415 USA
Phone: (423) 505-6911
Fax: (423) 267-9797
jason.hill@papercutinteractive.com
{82–83}

Kristina E. Kim
plus design, inc.
25 Drydock Ave.
Boston, MA 02210 USA
Phone: (617) 478-2470 x3001
Fax: (617) 478-2471
plus@plusdesigninc.com
{17, 50, 64, 128, 152, 194, 211}

Michael Crigler
Prank Design
9 Islington St.
Allston, MA 02134 USA
Phone: (617) 470-4097
dirkcrig@aol.com
{116}

Josh Williams
Pure Imagination Studios
P.O. Box 90355
Southlake, TX 76092 USA
Phone: (817) 741-2980
josh@pureimagination.com
{139, 144}

R
Lizá Defossez Ramalho
R2 Design
Praceta D Nuno Álvares Pereira 20 2o BZ
Matosinhos 4450 218
Portugal
Phone: +351 22 938 68 65
Fax: +351 22 938 68 65
r2@rdois.com
{95}

Curtis Achilles
Red Communications
155 Dalhousie St., Studio 524
Toronto, ON M5B 2P7
Canada
Phone: (416) 894-2733
Fax: (416) 214-9569
curtis@redcommunications.com
{20, 131}

Ida Cheinman
re: salzman designs
2304 E. Baltimore St.
Baltimore, MD 21224 USA
Phone: (410) 732-8379
ida.cheinman@verizon.net
{93, 147, 185}

Tim McGrath
Rick Johnson & Company
1120 Pennsylvania Ave.
Albuquerque, NM 87110 USA
Phone: (505) 266-1100
Fax: (505) 266-0525
tmcgrath@rjc.com
{147}

Greer Hutchinson
Riordon Design
131 George St.
Oakville, ON L6J 3B9
Canada
Phone: (905) 339-0750
Fax: (905) 339-0753
greer@riordondesign.com
{69, 160, 170}

Robert Palmer
Robert Palmer Design
2226 River Run Drive, #157
San Diego, CA 92018 USA
Phone: (619) 920-5460
robert9@san.rr.com
{128}

Susan Elliott
RocketDog Communications
100 S. King St., #580
Seattle, WA 98104 USA
Phone: (206) 254-0248
Fax: (206) 254-0238
susan@rocketdog.org
{198–199}

Ross Hogin
Ross Hogin Design
557 Roy St., Ste. 150
Seattle, WA 98109 USA
Phone: (206) 283-4445
Fax: (206) 283-2011
hogin@hogin.com
{29}

Jennifer Roycroft
Roycroft Design
3 Shawnee Circle
Andover, MA 01810 USA
Phone: (978) 475-4505
Fax: (978) 475-1455
jennifer@roycroftdesign.com
{19}

Justin Ahrens
Rule 29
25 S. Grove Ave., Ste. 301
Elgin, IL 60120 USA
Phone: (847) 717-4368
Fax: (847) 717-4372
justin@rule29.com
{85, 97, 130, 217}

S
Rudolph Widjajahakim
Sapulidi Advertising & Gift Promotion
Kepa Duri Mas Blok: MM no. 7
West Jakarta
DKI Jakarta 11510
Indonesia
Phone: +62-21-563-4182
Fax: +62-21-5696-3567
marketing@sapulidi.com
www.sapulidi.com
{188}

Sheree Clark
Sayles Graphic Design
3701 Beaver Ave.
Des Moines, IA 50310 USA
Phone: (515) 279-2922
Fax: (515) 279-0212
sayles@saylesdesign.com
{68, 84}

Josh Silverman
Schwadesign
337 Summer St., 3rd floor
Boston, MA 02210 USA
Phone: (617) 912-9434
Fax: (617) 912-9434
josh@schwadesign.com
{54}

Jacquelyn Rinaldi
Sciortino Advertising
4815 W. Russell Rd., #10-5
Las Vegas, NV 89118 USA
Phone: (702) 227-4144
Fax: (702) 227-4520
jacquelyn@sciortinoadvertising.com
{50}

Scott Love
Scott Love Design
11 Bates Road
Milton, MA 02186
Phone: (617) 696-6904
Fax: (617) 698-1485
scotlove@shore.net
{204–205}

Karen Simon
Simon Does, LLC
146 Bank St., Ste. 3A
New York, NY 10014 USA
Phone: (212) 924-7725
Fax: (212) 929-8905
karen@simondoes.com
{33}

Pia Kempter
Simon & Goetz Design
Darmstaedter Landstr. 180
Frankfurt 60598
Germany
Phone: +49 (0) 69-968855-0
Fax: +49 (0) 69-968855-23
p.kempter@simongoetz.de
{124–125, 126, 156}

Jennifer Stucker
SiSU Design
23906 E. Second St.
Grand Rapids, OH 43522 USA
Phone: (419) 832-6049
Fax: (419) 832-6049
sisu4u@adelphia.net
{144}

Ivy Wong
Splash Interactive
99 Harbour Square, Ste. 212
Toronto, ON M5J 2H2
Canada
Phone: (416) 460-0850
ivy@splashinteractive.com
{137}

Stereobloc
Schonhauser Allee 74a
Berlin 10437
Germany
Phone: +49 0 30 447310 13
Fax: +49 0 30 447310 17
info@stereobloc.de
www.stereobloc.de
{78, 94}

Anne Demphausse
Stormship Studios
34 Salem St.
Medford, MA 02155 USA
Phone: (781) 391-9517
anne@stormship.com
{195}

T
Josh Phillipson
Tesser
650 Delancy St., #404
San Francisco, CA 94107 USA
Phone: (415) 541-9999
Fax: (415) 541-9699
john.phillipson@tesser.com
{114}

Tino Schmidt
timespin–Digital Communications GmbH
Sophienstr. 7
Jena 07743
Germany
Phone: +49 0 3641 35970
info@timespin.de
{70}

Tom Sizu
Tom & John: A Design Collaborative
1475 15th St.
San Francisco, CA 94103 USA
Phone: (415) 621-6800
Fax: (415) 551-1220
tom@tom-john.com
{38, 76, 95, 148, 216}

Jan Tracy
Tracy Design
118 Southwest Blvd
Kansas City, MO 64108 USA
Phone: (816) 421-0606
Fax: (816) 421-0177
jantracy@swbell.net
{51, 58, 208–209}

U
David Hawkins, Glenn Howard
Untitled
Studio 6, The Lux Building
214 Horton Square
London N1 6NU
UK
Phone: +020 7613 3129
david@untitledstudio.com
{42–43, 109, 129}

Chris Parks
Up Design Bureau
209 E. William St., Ste. 1100
Wichita, KS 67202 USA
Phone: (316) 267-1546
Fax: (316) 267-3760
cp@updesignbureau.com
{49, 88, 94, 106, 131}

V
Fritz Klaetke
Visual Dialogue
4 Concord Square
Boston, MA 02118 USA
Phone: (617) 247-3658
Fax: (617) 247-3658
fritz@visualdialogue.com
{56, 110, 123}

Heike Hartmann
Visuelle Kommunikation
Birsteiner Str. 29
Frankfurt AM Main 60386
Germany
Phone: +49 (0) 69-499341
Fax: +49 (0) 69-48002514
hh@vk-ffm.de
{79}

Scott Carslake
Voice
74 Ridgehaven Dr.
Bellevue Heights, SA 5050
Australia
Phone: +618 8177 2171
Fax: +618 8177 2172
info@voicedesign.net
{29, 107, 133, 134}

W
Wendy Church
Wallace Church, Inc.
330 E. 48th St.
New York, NY 10017 USA
Phone: (212) 755-2903
Fax: (212) 355-6872
{168–169}

Peter Watts
Watts Design
66 Albert Rd.
South Melbourne, Victoria 3205
Australia
Phone: +61 (0) 3 9696 4116
peter@wattsdesign.com.au
{202, 211}

Williams and House
296 Country Club Rd.
Avon, CT 06001 USA
Phone: (860) 674-4140
Fax: (860) 675-4124
{89}

Paul Burgess
Wilson Harvey
Sir John Lyon House
High Timber St.
London EC4V 3NX
UK
Phone: +44 0 20 7420 7700
paulb@wilsonharvey.co.uk
{138, 155, 179}

Wing Chan
Wing Chan Design, Inc.
167 Perry St., 5C
New York, NY 10014 USA
Phone: (212) 727-9109
Fax: (212) 727-8742
wingchandesign.ny@verizon.net
www.wingchandesign.com
{23}

Colleen Carr
WomanDriven
P.O. Box 27652
San Diego, CA 92198-1652 USA
Phone: (858) 675-1015
Fax: (858) 485-9521
ccar@womandriven.com
{76}

Will Johnson
Wow! A Branding Company
101-1300 Richards St.
Vancouver, BC V6B 3G6
Canada
Phone: (604) 683-5655
Fax: (604) 683-5686
will@wowbranding.com
{142, 149, 158, 196, 216}

Thomas Fabian
Wunderburg Design
Innere Laufer Gasse 11
Nürnberg, Bavaria 90403
Germany
Phone: +49 911 23555420
Fax: +49 911 23555424
fabian@wunderburg-design.de
{24–25}

Z
Rachel Karaca
Zigzag Design
4006 Oak #3
Kansas City, MO 64111 USA
Phone: (816) 213-1198
Fax: (816) 931-2914
raka@uzigzag.com
{70}

Tew Sun Ne
Zucchini Design Pte. Ltd.
302 Mosque St.
Singapore 059508
Phone: +65 6887 5746
Fax: +65 6223 8070
sunne@zucchini.com.sg
{68, 166}

about the author: Blackcoffee specializes in brand development and communications for consumer brands. The Boston-based brand positioning and design firm was founded in 1994 by Mark Gallagher and Laura Savard. Focusing on the convergence of human factors and brand position, the firm transforms abstract problems into focused messages that resonate with consumers. Blackcoffee works with a wide range of national and international brands including Acura, Adidas/Salomon, Converse, Hasbro, Kryptonite, MTV, Showtime, Timberland, and Zildjian. This is the first book Blackcoffee has authored for Rockport Publishers. For more information about the firm visit WWW.BLACKCOFFEE.COM